POETS OF THE NICARAGUAN REVOLUTION

KATABASIS

REPUBLICA DE NICARAGUA

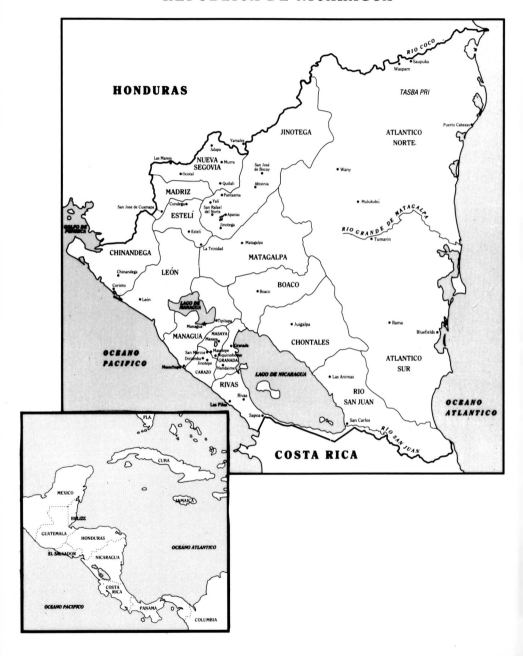

POETS

of the

NICARAGUAN

REVOLUTION

An Anthology

translated by Dinah Livingstone

Copyright of the poems remains with the authors 1993
Translation copyright: Dinah Livingstone 1993
First published 1993 by KATABASIS
10 St Martins Close, London NW1 0HR
Cover illustration: Tony Capellán
Cover design: Virman Man, Boldface, London (071 253 2014)
Disc output to laser: Daisywheel, Merseyside (051 630 2657)
Printed by SRP, Exeter (0296 29271)

ISBN: 0 904872 21 1
British Library Cataloguing-in-Publication Data.
A catalogue record for this book is available
from the British Library.

DEDICATION

These poems are witness to the time
when people struggling all over the world
were encouraged, not just by News from Nowhere,
but from Somewhere in Nicaragua.

The book and the song below are dedicated
in homage from London
to the people of Nicaragua
for their inspiration and generosity
and to a future Planetary Revolution.

SONG

Mistakes heartache
unexpected defeat
burnt all black
dead beat.

Fire charred the heath
death dried the heart.
They who hated this earth
have deeply scarred.

Yet deeper the seed
love sheds its life.
Blood stopped stone dead.
Moist warmth unfurls leaf.

My hope is red petal
heart beat.

Dinah Livingstone

ACKNOWLEDGMENTS

The translator and Katabasis wish to express our warmest thanks to Ernesto Cardenal, former Sandinista Minister of Culture, for permission and encouragement to publish this anthology, without which it could not have appeared. And above all, warmest thanks to the poets, to whom we shall always remain in debt. We are very grateful to be able to publish their work in this anthology at a time when the people of Britain hear very little about Nicaragua.

Thanks to the poet Julio Valle-Castillo for much help and advice with the anthology. Thanks to Robert Pring-Mill for his kindness and for sending copies of his invaluable critical articles.

Thanks to Anne Beresford and Kathleen McPhilemy for reading and criticising the translation, Christopher Hampton for criticising the introduction, Helen Yuill and Jorge López for helping with the chronology and Roberto Rivera-Reyes, María Eugenia Bravo Calderara, Grace Livingstone and Cicely Herbert for reading the proofs.

Some of the translations have previously appeared in *Gairfish, Tok, In the Shadow of Columbus* (Leicester-Masaya Link Group), *CIIR News, Nicaragua Today, Well Red.*

KATABASIS is grateful for the assistance of the Arts Council of Great Britain and the London Arts Board.

CONTENTS

Notes on the poets are in alphabetical order of surnames,
with notes on some of the poems under the author's name.
Anon is listed alphabetically under Anon.

INTRODUCTION

Shelley says in his *Defence of Poetry*:

> The most unfailing herald, companion and follower of the
> awakening of a great people to work a beneficial change in
> opinion or institution is Poetry. At such periods there is an
> accumulation of the power of communicating and receiving
> intense and impassioned conceptions respecting man and
> nature.

This is certainly true of the Nicaraguan Revolution, which produced
the most abundant flowering of poetry in Latin America this century.
Such wealth cannot possibly be contained in an anthology of this size.
A selection had to be made. I kept wanting to put more and more
poems in, until the book became so large I simply had to stop. The
Nicaraguan Atlantic Coast – an autonomous region with Indian groups
speaking their own languages and a black population often bi-lingual
in Spanish and English – is under-represented, although this anthology
does have the marvellous David Macfield. There is scope here for
other anthologies.

    The choice has been made from the large quantity of poetry
books – new work and re-issues – published by the Sandinista
Ministry of Culture and by Nicaraguan publishing houses, particularly
Editorial Nueva Nicaragua and Vanguardia, and also from a fat pile of
photocopies given to the translator by Ernesto Cardenal. Despite the
severe economic conditions faced by the Sandinista government,
culture was given a high priority, especially poetry. British poets may
feel envious to hear that Editorial Nueva Nicaragua regularly
published poetry in much larger editions than are common here (e.g.
Julio Valle-Castillo and Rosario Murillo each: 6,000; Daisy Zamora:
8000; Cardenal's *Cántico Cósmico*: 10,000; Ricardo Morales Avilés:
10,000; Gioconda Belli: 15,000.) There is also a breadth and
generosity of scope. Many new writers are published as well as
established poets. Not long after Rosario Murillo had publicly
criticised the work produced by the Ministry of Culture's cherished
poetry workshops, the Ministry of Culture published her collection *Un*

Deber de Cantar (June 1982). Both established and new poets were regularly published in *Ventana* and *Nuevo Amanecer Cultural*, the respective cultural supplements to the daily newspapers *Barricada* and *El Nuevo Diario* and in the magazine *Poesía Libre*.

For reasons of space, this anthology has tried to offer new material and avoid reproducing translations of poems published and readily available in England. (The notes mention other publications.) This has obviously meant omitting some famous poems, but Nicaragua has produced so much good poetry, that republishing extant translations would have meant losing the opportunity to give a wider selection an airing in England. On the few occasions when a poem previously published in this country has been included, the translation is different, except for Ernesto Cardenal's poem 'Final Offensive'.

One reason for including this poem was its reference at the end to Leonel Rugama's 'The Earth is a Satellite of the Moon'. Nicaragua is a small country with a population of not much more than 3 million (less than half that of London). Many of the poets know each other, are related, or fall in love with each other; they address poems to each other, speak about other poets or refer to other people's poems in their own. For example, Daisy Zamora writes a poem for 'Comandante Dos', Dora María Téllez, one of the leaders of the FSLN Assault on the National Palace in 1978, who has a love poem in this anthology. Daisy also writes a teasing love poem to Ernesto Cardenal. Ernesto Cardenal writes a poem to his nephew, Ernesto Castillo, a young combatant whose poems were found after he was killed in action. Gioconda Belli writes about looking for Ricardo Morales' tomb on a rainy day in the Diriamba cemetery, and not finding it. And while travelling in Hungary on a poetry tour, Julio Valle-Castillo remembers Bosco Centeno's poem about a fallen *guerrillero*, carrying maize cobs in his uniform pockets, which sprout from his body. When Julio hears a similar story about a Hungarian poet, he sends a postcard poem to Bosco. This cohesion has been one of the particular pleasures in compiling the anthology and it is hoped it will add to the reader's enjoyment too.

In complete contrast to the postmodernist atomisation that reduces poetry criticism and even poetry to a matter of style, the Revolution gave the Nicaraguan poets a common culture, a project, a language and a climate, in which they could speak and listen to each other, and also argue. Bitter arguments did break out, especially about the literary merit of the workshop poetry, which will be described below. However, because of their shared revolutionary experience and hopes, the simplest love poem acquires resonance from the most ambitious all-embracing work, such as Ernesto Cardenal's 581-page *Cosmic Canticle*, and vice versa.

*

Following a prologue set in the fifties, the body of the book offers a selection of thirty-five poets from the foundation of the Sandinista National Liberation Front (FSLN) in 1961, through the triumph of the Revolution in 1979 and the Sandinista decade in power, to their defeat in the 1990 elections. To give an idea of the story, the book follows a roughly chronological order, but to give the reader a better chance of catching an individual poet's voice, each poet's work is grouped together. This means that if a poet has been writing over a considerable period, the chronology is telescoped in his or her group of poems. This double, sometimes conflicting, ordering principle seemed better than any of the alternatives available for the book's purpose, which is to present these poems with enough of their context to make them accessible to English readers. An outline chronology and notes on the poets in alphabetical order – with notes on individual poems, when they occur, under the author's name – are given at the end. As the poems are very varied, it is hoped readers will read the book as a whole and also find their particular favourites.

The prologue has Ernesto Cardenal's epitaph for his friend Báez Bone killed in the April Conspiracy of 1954 against the dictator, in which Ernesto also took part. This is followed by an extract from the Last Letter to his Mother (cut up into lines and laid out as verse by Carlos Fonseca) from Rigoberto López Pérez, a poet who wanted to bring about the 'beginning of the end' by killing the first dictator Somoza, in 1956. There is also a small, later, poem by Ernesto Cardenal on 'The Pork that Rigoberto did not Eat'.

The body of the book begins with a dream-horses poem by Ana Ilce Gómez, a highly individual working class poet. Then the thirty-five poets chosen include some early student leaders and heroes and martyrs of the liberation struggle: the ex-seminarian Leonel Rugama killed in a famous shoot-out with the National Guard in Managua; Ricardo Morales Avilés, university teacher whose prose is nearly all political analysis and whose poems nearly all love poems to Doris Tijerino; Felipe Peña, the peasant poet from Solentiname killed during the Final Offensive in May 1979, whose poems are full of his intimate knowledge of the country with its birds and animals, as well as his feelings as a combatant – which include timidity. These poets are very different and it is interesting that the 'pope of letters' in the sixties and seventies, the literary editor of *La Prensa*, Pablo Antonio Cuadra (who later became the only well known Nicaraguan poet not to support the Revolution) published and encouraged Leonel Rugama but dismissed Ricardo Morales.[1] Ricardo's poems stream out in a rush of energy; they are raw and untidy, but both the British poets who read the translation to give an opinion on how the poems sounded in English, Anne Beresford and Kathleen McPhilemy, singled him out as particularly moving. His poems were mainly written in prison. Not surprisingly, a good deal more of the poetry written during the liberation struggle was also written in prison. Again there are strong contrasts. Daniel Ortega's 'In Prison' ends with his best-known lines:

> We missed
> Managua in
>   miniskirts.

The poem is a menacing compilation of dislocated thoughts and overheard scraps, conveying a sense of extreme pressure, whereas Tomás Borge's letter to his two-year old daughter lyrically expresses a serene faith.

    The two last mentioned poets were among those who became ministers in the Sandinista government. Daniel became President and Tomás became Minister of the Interior. Others who became 'acknowledged legislators' were Sergio Ramírez (Vice-President), Dora María Téllez (Minister of Health), Ernesto Cardenal (Minister of Culture) and Daisy Zamora (Vice Minister of Culture). Other poets who worked for the Sandinista government were Michèle Najlis, Gioconda Belli and Julio Valle-Castillo. All these have poems in this book. In his poem 'Cabinet Meeting' Ernesto Cardenal describes his feeling:

> And I think: how odd,
> how very odd. It's love.

The cabinet meeting for love of their neighbour.

In the heady days after the Triumph, the whole apparatus of
the dictator's state was abolished and everything had to be re-
invented. The new rulers were not professional politicians and they
tried to make the revolutionary society they had imagined become a
reality. As many of them were poets, they experienced the
extraordinary delight of having the opportunity to 'do' what they had
'seen', the excitement of *poesis* – making, a new society. In his poem
'The Past Will Not Return', euphoric with wordplay and incantatory
on a kind of grammatical 'high', Cardenal's uncle, José Coronel
Urtecho, veteran founder of the Vanguard Literary Movement in the
twenties, expresses how the Revolution 'makes all things new'. At the
same time the poet Luz Marina Acosta, an office worker in the new
Ministry of Culture, is thoroughly realistic (and humorous) about
some of the difficulties. With the Revolution there is a notable
increase in women poets. Poets feel freer to be funny and some of the
poems have deft light touches. Cony Pacheco, a nurse who became
one of the co-ordinators of the poetry workshops, is a particularly
piquant example in her 'Dear John' poem.

An oppressed and hungry peasantry does not simply want
'food aid', but the means to produce food for themselves, above all
land. The Sandinista government confiscated the dictator's estates,
and later some under-used large land-holdings, to redistribute them.
Likewise the new Ministry of Culture 'socialised the means of poetic
production' by setting up poetry workshops all over the country. Two
months after the Triumph, the first poetry workshop was established in
Monimbó, the Indian district of Masaya, 'because of what Monimbó
symbolises in this Revolution', says Cardenal. By 1982 at least sixty-
six workshops were meeting regularly throughout the country. As well
as publishing work by known Nicaraguan poets and poets from
abroad, the Ministry of Culture's magazine *Poesía Libre*, edited by
Julio Valle-Castillo, regularly published a section of poems from the
workshops,

The March 10th 1980 issue of the Sandinista newspaper
Barricada published Ernesto Cardenal's 'Rules' for writing poetry. We
quote them here extensively because they are interesting both for their
exotic bossiness and their substantial good sense, especially as advice
to new writers.[2] Cardenal gives seven 'Rules' and introduces them by

the remark, with which he clearly enjoys provoking the literary establishment: 'Writing good poetry is easy and the rules for doing it are few and simple.'

1.   Verse need not rhyme. If one line ends with *Sandino*, do not try to end another with *destino*; if one ends with *León* , there is no need to make another end in *corazón*. Rhyme is a good thing in songs and very suitable in slogans. E.g. 'We won in the rising. We shall win alphabetising'. But rhyme is not a good thing in modern poetry. Nor is it a good thing to have a regular rhythm (all the lines with the same number of syllables): verse should be completely free, with the lines long or short, as the poet chooses.

2.   We should prefer more concrete terms to vague ones. To say 'tree' is vaguer or more abstract than saying... *malinche* [flame tree], which is more concrete. 'Animal' is more abstract than 'iguana', 'rabbit'. And it is more abstract to say 'liquor' than to say 'whiskey', 'champagne'... Good poetry is usually made out of very concrete things.

3.   Poetry has an added appeal if it includes proper names: the names of rivers, towns, and villages. And people's names...

4.   Rather than being based on ideas, poetry needs to be based on things which reach us through the senses: which can be felt with the touch, which can be tasted with the palate, which can be heard, which can be seen, which can be smelt. It is good to make a point of saying that corrugated iron is 'rusty'... that an iguana is 'rough-skinned', that a macaw is 'red, yellow and blue' (and try to describe the sound a macaw makes). The most important images are visual ones: most things reach us through our eyes.

5.   We should write as we speak. With the natural plainness of the spoken language, not the written language. To put the adjective first, as in 'los sombríos senderos' [the shady paths] is not natural in our language, but rather: 'los senderos sombríos'. By the same token, it is preferable not to use *tú* but *vos* [i.e. for the

second person singular] in our Nicaraguan poetry, since that is
how we speak in daily life. The greater part of the new
Nicaraguan poetry is now using *vos*... (*Vos* is used in almost
all of Latin America, but there are few places where it is used
as much as in Nicaragua; the new Nicaraguan poetry is going
to impose the use of *vos* throughout Latin America.)

6. Avoid what are called commonplaces, clichés, or hackneyed
    expressions. In other words, whatever has gone on being
    repeated in the same way for a long time. For example
    'burning sun', 'icy cold', 'cruel tyrant'... The poet should try
    to discover new ways of putting things; if what he writes is
    made up of expressions blunted by use, it is not poetry.

7. Try to condense the language as much as possible. In other
    words, to abridge. All words that are not absolutely necessary
    should be left out. If there are two ways of putting something,
    one should choose the shorter... A poem may be a very long
    one, but each of its lines should be in very condensed
    language.

With reference to point 7, Cardenal's own latest work the *Cántico
Cósmico* is *very* long, but it is true to say the style is succinct even if
not 'telegraphic', a commendatory adjective he adopted from Ezra
Pound. As for point 4, of course Cardenal's poems are full of ideas
and musings, but he usually approaches the idea through 'very
concrete things'.

About the use of the popular second person pronoun *vos*, as
Robert Pring-Mill[3] says, it is going a bit far to proselytise for its use
in poetry throughout Latin America, when it is not common usage in
some countries. However, as a foreign visitor to Nicaragua, I have to
admit to feeling much more thrilled the first time a Nicaraguan friend
addressed me as 'vos' than by a 'tu' from any Latin country in
Europe. The actual sentence was a joking '¿Vos querés pelear
conmigo?' [Do you want to quarrel with me?] With the stress on the
last syllable of the verb, and the Nicaraguan slightly velar fricative
quality to the final 's', so that 'vos' almost rhymes with Scottish
'loch', the effect was so appealing that I could not possibly want to
quarrel with it. One of the most striking uses of the word 'vos' in

Nicaraguan verse, stating the fundamental premise of liberation theology in the simplest possible way, is the opening line of Carlos Mejía Godoy's *Peasant Mass* (which unavoidably loses its savour in translation): 'You are the God of the poor'; here 'vos' challenges the the conquistadors' and present-day oppressors' claim to have God on their side by invoking a God who stands in intimate solidarity with the oppressed: 'Vos sos el Dios de los pobres.'

The name Cardenal gives to the kind of poetry he is recommending is 'exteriorist', which he had earlier defined as:[4]

> 'Exteriorism' is a word created in Nicaragua to describe the type of poetry we prefer. Exteriorism is neither an *ism* nor a literary school. It is as ancient as Homer and biblical poetry (in fact, it is what has constituted the great poetry of every age).

> Exteriorism is poetry created by images of the outside world, the specific world of poetry... exteriorism is objective poetry: narrative and anecdotal, made from the elements of real life and particular things, with proper names and precise details and exact dates and figures and facts and sayings. In sum, it is *impure poetry*. Poetry that for some is nearer to prose than to poetry, and which has mistakenly been called 'prosy', because its subject matter is as wide as that of prose.

In March 1981 *Ventana* ran a debate on the merit of the workshop poetry. The first article was published from the editorial board, chaired by Rosario Murillo and including Gioconda Belli. (Possibly these mainly young but recognised poets were not entirely free from a touch of exclusiveness.) They argued that 'exteriorism' limited poetic creativity and was becoming an 'official style'. Other complaints were that the workshop poets were encouraged to write only on revolutionary subjects and that they painted too rosy a picture of the revolution.

Sixty-six poets and organisers of workshops replied to these criticisms. As poems were brought to workshops after being written, they said, the themes could not be prescribed, but many poets were interested in revolutionary themes, because the revolution had affected all their lives so recently. They added a list of the wide variety of subjects treated in the workshop poetry published in *Poesía Libre*. They declared[5]:

> We are the people: cobblers, domestic workers, children of artisans, bakers, clothes-sellers, agricultural labourers, students, Sandinista police, soldiers, militia members; a doctor from Jinotega, members of the Sandinista Air Force, peasants from Río San Juan, Palacagüina, San Juan de Oriente...

They accused the *Ventana* editors of criticising them in 'a confused and pretentious language, whereas we speak the simple language of our people'. The editors replied that the workshop poetry is 'a uniform poetic creation that could be read as the work of a single person'. Gioconda Belli wrote an article attacking Mayra Jiménez, the first workshop organiser, for imposing new limitations on creativity in the name of the revolution. The workshops then found a venerable champion in the Grand Old Man of Nicaraguan poetry, José Coronel Urtecho, who declared that some, though not of course all, the workshop poetry was of excellent quality. The unique virtue of the workshop movement was that the government was making it possible for everyone to learn how to exercise their talent for poetry. The project was only just beginning and eventually it would lead to the creation of some first class poets and readers of poetry in Nicaragua and to 'other benefits which are not even imaginable at the moment'.

In retrospect from a decade later, on the evidence of the workshop poetry translated here, the charge that this poetry is 'all the same' and could have been written by one person has become patently untrue. Of course with the revolution, quantities of quite ordinary little poems were produced by people who would never have dreamed of writing poetry before. This did wonders for their self-respect, especially if they had only just learned to write. But compared, for example, to the poems inside the average British greetings card or in a paper like *Woman's Own*, they were, as Cardenal claimed, 'good modern poetry'. And gradually, interesting and distinct voices emerged.

Cony Pacheco's sharp humour has already been mentioned. One of the other workshop organisers, the carpenter Carlos Calero, has a luminous poem describing 'Lake Masaya' with its fishermen and washerwomen, who use the traditional Indian cypress root for soap. At the end of the day the poet sees a line of women going up the gully carrying other people's washing on their heads (still! – hardly idealising the revolution):

> and you catch the smell of cypress root
> the smell of woman.

Gerardo Gadea describes the cadets coming to the military school, who are 'like birds when winter comes' (i.e. when it rains after the long dry summer). The poem starts with a bugle-bird trilling on the branch of a flame tree, which has just burst into scarlet blossom. The simile above all conveys the *buoyancy* of the recruits at this stage. Another simile from the Solentiname peasant poet Iván Guevara (now a captain in the Sandinista army) compares a girl who 'did not come back to the camp' with a rabbit he saw while on guard, which did not reappear either and makes his disgruntled disappointment palpable. Belli had accused Mayra Jiménez of trying to stamp out figures of speech in the workshop poetry. Even if this were true – which is doubtful – she clearly did not succeed. The other workshop organiser represented here, Juan Ramón Falcón, has an interesting poem in which he conveys the shock of accidentally recognising a dead girl friend – a *guerrillera* – on television. She is running with her gun and he detects her through the black and red scarf masking her face. He manages to convey the strangeness of seeing her iconised on video.

Even two of the simplest workshop poems have a strongly personal quality. Isidro Tercero, a pseudonym because he belongs to the Sandinista security service, is miffed when a girlfriend, who has learnt to accept his rapid comings and goings on duty, now sounds a little too unruffled when he has to leave again and she says: 'Of course, comrade!' A pleasantly insecure poem from a man with such a macho job! Lesbia Rodríguez pats her large belly and talks to her unborn child, who in turn will have more children, so she will get older and Nicaragua younger. Perhaps the most 'formulaic' of these simple poems here is the young literacy teacher, Martha Blandino's 'Narciso', addressed to her adult pupil. Her poem's saving grace is its nervous uncertainty, developing into very mixed feelings when it is time for her to leave.

Ernesto Cardenal defended the workshops in his closing speech to the Harvard Congress on Disarmament and Peace on 2nd

May 1981.[6] He denounces US foreign policy. But 'we do not confuse the North American people with imperialism. The best of this people are with us.' Then he summons the names of many great US poets who would be with the Revolution, and says their work is studied in the Nicaraguan poetry workshops. He describes some of the poems produced by workshop poets in the Army and concludes:

> All these poets in our Armed Forces were combatants in the Revolution, that is, they were combatants for love. And they are ready to fight again at any moment to defend this Revolution, just as the whole Nicaraguan people are also ready. But they hope too that one day arms will not be necessary. Until that day comes let us struggle for disarmament and arms control. And let us hope that in other armies there will also be poetry and song as in Nicaragua. We can offer other armies advice in matters of poetry.

Obviously the question occurs as to whether Cardenal's preference for 'exteriorism' is related to the fact that he is a catholic priest and therefore less likely to write about his private life. I think there is an element of truth in this and in some of his public poems Cardenal's role is that of the *chilan*, the wise priest-seer he evokes in his *Homage to the American Indians*. Nevertheless, he can be outspoken about former girlfriends. On one occasion in Hamburg[7] a girl in the audience at a poetry reading sharply recalls a former affair. (He returns to his hotel and bites into an apple.) One of the themes of the whole *Cosmic Canticle* and in particular, *Cantiga* 41 entitled 'Song of Songs' in which 'the whole universe is a wedding', is the celebration of erotic love as the energy and delight of the universe. The *Cantiga* is very sensuous. Cardenal definitely has an 'interiorist' side.

So do many other of the Nicaraguan poets and there are no restrictions on their 'confessing', when they wish. It is the personal element that gives bite and individuality to many of the simplest poems. Their love poems are not coy and usually written in the first person. Lesbia Rodríguez describes making love with a man she meets while billeted away from home as a literacy teacher, who 'asked me if I felt cold', a somewhat naff chat-up line, which seems to have amused her. She concludes candidly: 'And I don't regret it'. The women poets who flourished with the Revolution provide a new dimension to the poetry, not so much 'interiorist' as 'incarnate'. They express how it feels to be in their – female – bodies. Again their styles are very different. Rosario Murillo, chair of the *Ventana* editorial board that criticised the workshop poetry, clearly does not feel bound by the ministerial 'Rules'. She can be both prolix and abstract but the beginning of her poem included here, 'Woman in the Revolution', strikingly conveys how she *sees* differently when she has a period, and how this bodily revolution affects her work in the Revolution. Gioconda Belli's style is effusive and passionate, charged with rhythmic energy. Watching her daughter standing with others at a ceremony, she feels the square is like 'a huge womb giving birth'. On the other hand in a poem that speaks 'with the natural plainness of the spoken language', though full of emotion as well as external detail and proper names, Luz Marina Acosta, working in the Ministry of Culture whose offices were set up in a grand old house that had belonged to the dictator, makes us feel how she is

> nauseated by the clean, white lavatories
> and cold bathrooms in this house that was Somoza's.

In language that is also bare and limpid, Vidaluz Meneses' poem 'Voluntary Work' appeals directly to the senses, sometimes more than one at once. Having left her office in the city to go and help with the harvest, she relates how:

> We women recall the months of pregnancy
> as we tie the baskets to our waists
> and gradually increase their weight
> by filling them with coffee.

This image also works in reverse: we women who can recall the months of pregnancy feel what it is like to be a coffee picker.

Although many poems written directly after the Triumph are understandably euphoric, as the decade develops there is no lack of poems on painful subjects. Carlos Martínez Rivas, a poet in his sixties, from the same generation as Cardenal, vituperates the Church hierarchy. The archbishop of Managua, Obando y Bravo, had eventually supported the bourgeois opposition against the dictator, but loathed the Sandinistas. (For this reason, they sometimes found him a useful mediator, when it was essential not to have someone who could be accused of partiality towards them.) Not long after the Pope visited Nicaragua in 1983, where he insulted the mothers of Contra victims, and insulted Ernesto Cardenal (for being a Minister in the Sandinista government), he appointed Obando y Bravo as the only cardinal in Central America. Carlos Martínez' poem 'Welcome, Monseñor' is a blisteringly sarcastic attack on Obando on this occasion. Gioconda Belli's torrential 'Nicaragua Water Fire' is an outpouring of defiance, a magnificent rant of resistance at the height of Reagan's war and blockade. The poem also picks up Ana Ilce Gómez' image of dream-horses. Julio Valle-Castillo's 'Ballad of the Deserter' is a remarkably tender poem about a terrified deserting conscript from the Sandinista army, buried without military honours after he is blown up by a North American mine. (It was thought that the promise to end conscription was a major vote catcher for the UNO opposition to the FSLN.) Finally Vidaluz Meneses' poem on the 1990 election defeat, 'Wailing Wall', is a heartbroken 'crying for the kingdom we have not been able to build'.

The epilogue has two poems. One is the first extant Nicaraguan poem, 'Song of the Nicaraguas', a lament written anonymously in Nahuatl in the sixteenth century at the time of the Spanish Conquest. The second is a 'cosmic' poem by Ernesto Cardenal, 'The Guerrilla's Tomb', which was the original title of the first poem in this anthology, his epitaph for Báez Bone. That poem ended with the famous line: 'What they did was bury a seed'. The anthology has a prose postscript by Sergio Ramírez, taken from his *Confession of Love*.[8] From the bitterness of defeat, he reaches out again to this seed image of hope. Against 'the arrogant exaltation of the definitive triumph of capitalism throughout the planet' proclaiming the end of history, he insists: 'The Latin American utopia is only just beginning to be born'. [9]

As during this whole period Nicaragua was under extreme pressure, it may be asked why poetry was considered so important. In England many literary editors regard political poetry as aesthetically suspect and vice versa, very few political papers or periodicals regularly publish poetry, because they do not take it seriously. However, during the Nicaraguan liberation struggle poetry and song had a crucial role in raising consciousness. As many combatants were poets, they told people what they were fighting for in their poems.

Poetry was regarded as a 'weapon loaded with the future', because it not only described things as they were but imagined how they could be. With the Triumph of the Revolution, the new government had many poets in it and many others occupied positions where they had a role in shaping the new society. In an ongoing process, they wanted a society that not only eliminated injustices but also created space for a 'new human being' to develop. This could not be done merely by handing out 'benefits' to the people, but required the population – ordinary human beings – to have the means to create themselves. Satisfaction of material needs was obviously a necessary condition for this to be possible, but from the earliest days of the revolution, culture was regarded as equally necessary. In particular, literacy and poetry. In Ernesto Cardenal's words,[10] 'Nicaragua's cultural liberation has been part of the struggle for national liberation.'

Nicaraguan culture had been devalued and regarded as inferior to the imported US culture. The poetry of the Revolution was quite often about the recent or present struggle. Poems about heroes and martyrs kept them *present* in the public awareness and encouraged people not to give in. For example, in Gioconda Belli's poem 'It happened one Sunday on a Trip to the Beach', when she cannot find Ricardo Morales' tomb in the Diriamba cemetery, it is 'like knocking on your door and not finding you in':

> And you still hurry about there,
> walking the wet streets,
> working and not dying ever.

But although this *remembering* matters very much, poetry giving details about everyday life is considered just as important. In a successful poem, the intractable particularity is given value and self-respect. This is especially the case with the peasant poems' intimate knowledge of the country and with love poems, that confide very personal experience and are addressed to individuals, sometimes by name. The stress on the senses and the particular, in Cardenal's 'Rules for Writing Poetry' and in the poetry workshops, connects with this revolutionary project of recovery of self-esteem both by Nicaragua as a national culture and by social classes previously despised as 'uncultured'. Cardenal contrasts this with what makes bad poetry. 'Certainly there is a lot of bad poetry in the whole of Latin America, often also on revolutionary subjects, poems to Che for example, with very good intentions but *full of rhetoric.*'[11]

In good poetry, the most particular often has the most universal resonance. Sergio Ramírez also points out[12] that paradoxically, a search for authenticity in revolutionary culture must take Nicaraguans well beyond their national frontiers. Finding authenticity does not mean solipsistically locking ourselves into our own vernacular or folklore, he says. Indeed as well as 'workshopping' poems, people attending the poetry workshops spent a lot of time reading poems by well known Nicaraguan poets and poets from other countries. *Poesía Libre* consistently published foreign poetry in translation as well as 'established' and 'workshop' Nicaraguan poetry. A national cultural identity did not imply narcissism and 'new human beings' reclaimed the culture of the whole human race, belonging to them as 'planetary citizens'.

This philosophy is, in Tomás Borge's words,[13] 'concerned with an integrative and kindly humanism, which considers the liberation of humanity as the basic objective of culture... Creating this new being for the citizens of the twenty-first century will be our most valuable contribution to humanity.' Poetry has long been held in high esteem in Nicaragua and just as in England we might address a person as 'Doctor', it is quite usual for Nicaraguans to use 'Poet' as a title or form of address, such as: '*Poeta*, how are you?'. Shortly after July 19th 1979, rapturous graffiti appeared on the walls of León:[14] 'The Triumph of the Revolution is the Triumph of Poetry'. Shelley would have liked that.

The anthology is bi-lingual, partly in order to be useful to Spanish speakers in this country who cannot easily get hold of the Nicaraguan books. Others may like to compare the Spanish and English texts. The translator will be grateful to receive any suggestions for improvements in future editions. Translating poetry is notoriously difficult. The poem has to come alive in the new language. Some poems that I liked in the original Spanish I found myself unable to translate into a living body of English, so these were not included. Punch lines are particularly difficult (as well as unfashionable in contemporary English poetry). As a minimum I wanted the translations to sound like poems in English when spoken aloud. The intention is to reverse what was long ago denounced by Nicaragua's revered poet Rubén Dario (1867-1916):[15]

15

Shall we be delivered to the fierce barbarians?
We are so many millions. Must we speak English?

The purpose of this anthology is to enable English-speakers, who do not want to be fierce barbarians, to *listen* to the Nicaraguan poets.

Dinah Livingstone
July 1993

NOTES

1. In an interview with Margaret Randall in *Risking a Somersault in the Air* (San Francisco 1984: this book has interviews with many of the poets in the anthology), Carlos José Guadamuz expresses his disgust at Cuadra's rejection of Morales' poems, whom he describes as 'one of the greatest intellectuals our country has produced'. 'He literally threw Ricardo's work at Doris... he told her: "This is no good. I can't publish this stuff." For Pablo Antonio Cuadra's point of view, see the interview with him in T. Cabastrero, *Leonel Rugama. El Delito de tomar la vida en serio*, (Editorial Nueva Nicaragua, Managua 1990), p. 434f. He says that where their martyrs are concerned, FSLN supporters do not distinguish between good and bad poets.

2. The translation of the 'Rules' is mainly taken, with some abbreviations, from Robert Pring-Mill, 'The "Workshop Poetry" of Sandinista Nicaragua', *Antilia* (Trinidad) 1/2, 1984, pp. 7-38.

3. Robert Pring-Mill, 'The "Workshop Poetry"...', *op. cit.* 1984.

4. Ernesto Cardenal, Prologue to the 1st edition of his anthology *Poesía Nicaragüense* (reprinted in 2nd Nicaraguan edition, Editorial Nueva Nicaragua, Managua 1986).

5. Quoted in Karyn Hollis, *Poesía del Pueblo para el pueblo* (San José de Costa Rica 1991). This book gives Cardenal's 'Rules' in Spanish and discusses the workshop debate in detail.

6. Ernesto Cardenal, 'La Paz Mundial y la Revolución de Nicaragua'. Speech given at the University of Harvard, closing the Congress on Disarmament and Peace, 2nd May 1981 (Managua 1981).

7. 'Apparition in Hamburg' is translated by D.L. in *Nicaraguan New Time* (Journeyman Press, London 1988).

8. Title essay in Sergio Ramírez, *Confesión de Amor* (Nicarao, Managua 1991).

9. 'El nacimiento de la utopía' in *Confesión de Amor, op. cit.* 1991.

10. Ernesto Cardenal, 'La Democratización de la cultura'. Speech given to UNESCO, April 1982. Quoted in *Poesía del Pueblo..., op. cit.* 1991.

11. Ernesto Cardenal, Introduction to *Talleres de Poesía*, anthology edited by Mayra Jiménez, (Ministry of Culture, Managua 1986).

12. Sergio Ramírez, *Balcanes y volcanes*, quoted in *Poesía del Pueblo..., op. cit.* 1991.

13. Tomás Borge, speech given in Spain in the summer of 1990. Translated in *1992 and the New World* (Leicester-Masaya Link Group, Leicester 1992).

14. Quoted in the concluding sentence to the introduction to Francisco de Asis Fernández (ed.), *Poesía política nicaragüense* (Ministry of Culture, Managua 1986).

15. From 'Los cisnes' in Rubén Darío, *Poesía* (Havana 1989).

PROLOGUE

1954-6

EPITAFIO PARA LA TUMBA
DE ADOLFO BAEZ BONE

Te mataron y no nos dijeron
      dónde enterraron tu cuerpo,
pero desde entonces todo el territorio nacional
      es tu sepulcro,
o más bien: en cada plano del territorio nacional en que
          no está tu cuerpo,
tú resucitaste.

¡Creyeron que te mataban
      con una orden de fuego!
Creyeron que te enterraban
y lo que hacían era enterrar una semilla.

1954

ERNESTO CARDENAL

EPITAPH FOR THE TOMB
OF ADOLFO BAEZ BONE

They killed you and did not tell us
    where they buried your body,
but from now on all our national territory
    is your grave,
or rather: in any part of it where
      your body is not,
you have risen again.

They thought they were killing you
    with their order to fire!
They thought they were burying you
but what they did was bury a seed.

1954

RIGOBERTO LÓPEZ PÉREZ

CARTA-TESTAMENTO

San Salvador, septiembre 4 de 1956
Señora Soledad López
León, Nicaragua

Mi querida mamá:
                    Aunque usted nunca lo ha sabido,
yo
        siempre
                he andado tomando parte
                                        en todo
lo que se refiere
                a atacar
                        el régimen funesto
                        de nuestra patria
y en vista
            de que todos los esfuerzos
                                    han sido inútiles
para tratar
            de lograr que
                        Nicaragua
                        vuelve a ser
                        (o lo sea por primera vez)
una patria libre,
sin afrentas y sin manchas,
                    he decidido,
                        aunque
                                mis compañeros

RIGOBERTO LÓPEZ PÉREZ

LAST LETTER TO HIS MOTHER

San Salvador, 4th September 1956
Señora Soledad Lopez
León, Nicaragua

My dear Mother:
                        Although you never knew it,
I
        have always
                been involved
                                        in everything
to do with
                attacking
                        the horrible regime
                        in our country
and seeing
                all those efforts
                                        have been useless
in order to try
                and succeed in making
                        Nicaragua
                        return to being
                (or rather become for the first time)
a free country,
without shame or blemish,
                        I have decided,
                        although
                                my comrades

23

no querían aceptarlo,
    el tratar de ser
      yo
        el que inicie
el principio del fin
de esa tiranía.

Si Dios quiere
    que perezca en mi intento,
no quiero
   que se culpe a nadie
      absolutamente,
pues todo ha sido
decisión mía...

Espero
  que tomará
    todas estas cosas
      con calma
y que debe pensar que lo que
      yo
       he hecho
es un deber
que cualquier
nicaragüense
que de veras
quiera
a su patria
   debía
   haber llevado a cabo
   hace mucho tiempo.
Lo mío

did not want to accept it,
                              to try to be
                                            the one
                                                  who initiates
the beginning of the end
of this tyranny.

If God wills
                  that I perish in my attempt
I do not want
                  anyone at all
                              to be blamed,
because it has been
entirely my decision...

I hope
            you will
                        take all these things
                                                  calmly
and think what
                        I
                              have done
is a duty
any
Nicaraguan
who really
loves
their country
                        should have
                        performed
                        a long time ago.
What I have done

no ha sido sacrificio
>> sino un deber
>> que espero haber cumplido.

Si usted
> toma las cosas como
>> yo
>> lo deseo
>>> le digo
>>> que me sentiré feliz.

Así es que
> nada de tristeza,
>> que el deber
>> que se cumple
>> con la patria

es la mayor satisfacción
que debe llevarse
un hombre de bien
>> como
>>> yo
>>> he tratado de serlo.

Si toma
> las cosas
>> con serenidad
>>> y con la idea absoluta de que

he cumplido
con mi más alto deber de
nicaragüense
>> le estaré
>>> muy agradecido.

Su hijo
> que siempre
>> la quiso mucho.

has not been a sacrifice
        but a duty
        which I hope to have fulfilled.
If you
    take things

         the way
         I hope you will
           I assure you
           I shall feel happy.
So

     no sadness,
       because serving
       the country
       in this way
is the greatest possible
satisfaction
to a decent man
     as I

      have tried
       to be.
If you take
   things
    serenely
     and are absolutely convinced
I have fulfilled
my highest duty
as a Nicaraguan,
   I shall be
     very grateful.
Your son
   who has always
     loved you very much.

ERNESTO CARDENAL

EL CHANCHO QUE
NO COMIO RIGOBERTO

Me contaron esto hace tiempo, me lo contó uno
al que se lo contó otro al que
   se le contó otro
    que fue testigo:
y es que Rigoberto López Pérez llegó
   al Parque Central de León
el 21 de septiembre de 1956, en la tardecita,
    y allí vió unos amigos,
y compró un chancho frito
y se puso a comer el chancho con yuca
      en una hoja de plátano,
pero casi no comió nada, sólo unos dos bocados,
no tenía hambre,
y tiró el chancho con yuca al suelo
     con la hoja,
y vió a un obrero muy borracho, y a un mendigo,
y dijo: 'Esto se va a acabar ya.'
    Y se fue para donde tenía que ir.

ERNESTO CARDENAL

THE PORK THAT RIGOBERTO DID NOT EAT

Some time ago I was told this by someone
who was told it by someone who was told it
     by someone else
         who was a witness:
that Rigoberto López Pérez arrived
     in the León Central Park
on 21st September 1956, in the afternoon,
        and there he met some friends,
and bought some fried pork
and began eating the pork with yucca
            in a plantain leaf,
but he hardly ate anything, just a couple of mouthfuls,
he was not hungry,
and he threw the pork and yucca on the ground
           together with the leaf,
and he saw a very drunk worker, and a beggar,
and he said: 'This is going to stop now.'
        And he went off where he had to go.

POETS
OF THE
NICARAGUAN REVOLUTION

1961-1990

LOS OCULTOS LIMITES

Los poemas son como caballos salvajes
sueltos en la pradera.
Un buen día uno va al campo y los descubre
en medio de los árboles
        trotando
         o haciendo el amor.

Estos caballos indomables
atraviesan tus sueños.
Sueltan las negras crines en medio
        de la noche.
Cruzan por tu vigilia relinchando.
Se agrupan en manadas inmensas
en el fondo del bosque
desde donde te arrojan
a los ciegos espacios del incendio.

Caballos cimarrones
animales de mito
        angeles
         centauros que me agitan.
Rompan la negra selva
los cercos brutales
los ocultos límites.
Tengo para ustedes hierba fresca
manchones de agua clara
montoncitos de alfalfa.
Vengan a pastar a mi página blanca.

ANA ILCE GÓMEZ

THE HIDDEN LIMITS

Poems are like wild horses
loose in the pasture.
One day you go to the country and find them
among the trees
                trotting about
                or making love.

These unbroken horses
gallop through your dreams.
They toss their black manes
                in the depths of the night.
They neigh in your sleep.
They gather in huge herds
in the heart of the forest
and fling you far
into fire that is blind.

Runaway horses
mythical animals
                angels
                centaurs that shake me.
Break through the dark wood
the brutal fences
the hidden limits.
I have fresh grass for you
pools of clear water
stacks of alfalfa.
Come and graze on my white page.

EPIGRAMA

Un Capitán G.N. que tiene su cuartel
      en una de estas ciudades
me mandó un Telegrama a mí
diciéndome que ni les entendía,
      ni le gustaban a él
los versos que yo escribo en *La Prensa*.
Yo creo que hasta el momento
ningún Poeta ha recibido mejor elogio.

FERNANDO SILVA

EPIGRAM

A National Guard captain whose barracks
      are in one of these cities
sent me a Telegram
telling me he neither understood
      nor liked
the verses I write in La Prensa.
I think this is the best praise
any Poet ever had.

FERNANDO GORDILLO

EL PRECIO DE LA PATRIA

3.000.000 es el precio de una Patria,
si alguien quiere venderla.
Y hubo quien quiso y la vendió.
Más tarde dijeron que sus hijos
nacieron para cantarla.
Como si la lucha no es el más alto
de los cantos.

Y la muerte el más grande.

FERNANDO GORDILLO

A COUNTRY'S PRICE

3,000,000 is the price of a country,
if anyone wants to sell it.
And someone did want to and did.
Later they said her children
were born to sing it.
As if the struggle were not the highest
of songs.

And death the greatest.

MICHÈLE NAJLIS

NOS PERSIGUIERON EN LA NOCHE

Nos persiguieron en la noche,
nos acorralaron
sin dejarnos más defensa que nuestras manos
unidas a millones de manos unidas.
Nos hicieron escupir sangre,
nos azotaron;
llenaron nuestros cuerpos con descargas eléctricas,
y nuestras bocas las llenaron de cal;
nos dejaron noches enteras junto a las fieras,
nos arrojaron en sótanos sin tiempos,
nos arrancaron las uñas;
con nuestra sangre cubrieron hasta sus tejados,
hasta sus propios rostros,
pero nuestras manos
siguen unidas a millones de manos unidas.

1966

MICHÈLE NAJLIS

THEY HUNTED US AT NIGHT

They hunted us at night
they cornered us
leaving us with no other defence but our hands
joined to millions more joined hands.
They made us spit blood,
they beat us;
they riddled our bodies with electric shocks,
and filled our mouths with lime;
they left us all night with wild beasts,
they threw us into timeless cellars,
they pulled out our finger nails;
they covered even their roof-tiles with our blood,
even their own faces,
but our hands
are still joined to millions more joined hands.

1966

SERGIO RAMÍREZ

DESPUES QUE HAYAS HUIDO

Con los dientes de la fiera clavados en el lomo
un hombre huye.
Huye bajo la noche manando sangre
regándola sobre las piedras
gimiendo hasta la sordera
va huyendo de algo.
Las fieras acechan tras su rastro
lo persiguen tenazmente
no le dejan
van a descuartizarlo
van a dejar sus huesos blancos
brillando a la luna.

¡Dios Santo no le dejan!
lo tienen cercado
ahora se le lanzan encima
y sus gemidos son terribles.

Gime el hombre bajo las estrellas
y su sangre se derrama sobre las piedras
su agonía va de grito en grito
y las fieras levantan sus cabezas
en la señal de la victoria.

– 'Logró evadirse,'
para los boletines oficiales.

SERGIO RAMÍREZ

AFTER YOU FLED

With the wild beast's teeth snapping at his back
a man flees.
Into the night he flees pouring with blood
raining blood onto the stones
his roars are deafening
he is running away from something.
The beasts hunt him
they pursue him tenaciously
they will not let him go
they are going to tear him to pieces
they are going to leave his white bones
shining in the moonlight.

Oh God, they won't let him go!
They have surrounded him
now they pounce
and his cries are terrible.

The man howls under the stars
and his blood spills on the stones
his agony screams and screams
and the beasts lift their heads
in sign of victory.

– 'He managed to escape,'
say the official bulletins.

41

– 'Huyó de noche por la frontera
lo persiguieron pero logró huir.'

En los secretos avisos del pueblo:
– 'Está a salvo, gracias a Dios,
está a salvo.'

Está a salvo,
está a salvo.

– 'He fled at night to the frontier
they chased him but he managed to get away.'

In the people's secret news:
– 'He is safe, thank God,
he is safe.'

He is safe,
he is safe.

EN LA PRISION

Patéalo así, así
en los güevos, en la cara,
en las costillas.
     Pasá el chuzo, la verga de toro,
hablá, hable hijueputa,
a ver el agua con sal,
hablaaaá, que no te queremos joder...
– Honorabilísimo y Reverendísimo
     arzobispo,
Excelentísimo e Ilustrísimo
     embajador.
La paz, el respeto a la persona,
la abundancia, la democracia.
Apriétenle las esposas
métanlo en la Chiquita
te vas a comer tu propia
mierda cabrón.

– La cucaracha, la cucaracha
ya no puede caminar
porque le falta, porque le falta
una pata para andar.
     La mierda y los orines,
chocho, cuánta gente.
Cabo de celda
que nadie hable con ese hombre,
que chuponée, que duerma en el suelo
y si hace un mate garrotéelo.

DANIEL ORTEGA

IN PRISON

Kick him like that, like that
in the balls, in the face
in the ribs.
            Give him the whip, the bull's poker,
talk, *talk* you bastard,
try the salt water,
ta-a-alk, it's not that we want to fuck you up...
– Most Honourable and Reverend
            archbishop,
Most Excellent and Illustrious
            ambassador.
Peace, respect for the person,
abundance, democracy.
Press the handcuffs tighter,
put him in La Chiquita
you're going to eat
your own shit you swine.

– *La cucaracha, la cucaracha*:
little cockroach can't walk now
because she's lacking, because she's lacking –
she's lost one leg so tell me how?
            Shit and piss,
God, what a crush.
Cell chief orders
no one talk to that man,
let him slobber, sleep on the floor
and if he tries anything garrot him.

– Las galeras, Auschwitz, Buchenwald,
Nicaragua.
A continuación, hoy 4 de julio
el aguerrido (se despachó un montón de negros)
Agregado Militar (Black Flag los mata al vuelo
        y los remata en el suelo)
condecorará
a los heroicos y caballerosos
        soldados.
        Soropeta, Juan Pluma, El Dormido,
        Casachica – te fuiste y me dejaste
        en la prisión
        tan sólo que me juzgaste
        como un ladrón –
Toro Nuevo, el Burrito, el Zopilote
el As Negro,
        la Chupeta
llega la Chupeta.
        La Caleta, a peso el polvo
este chavo es pura uva.
        – Si me das comida me culiás,
por tres cigarros la mamo.
La luna, los lirios, Dios,
el poeta apolítico.
– Por aqui pasó una pava
tan chiquita y voladora,
en el pico lleva flores
y en las alas sus amores.
        – Ayer me jalé un radio.
        Sí, tengo diez años
        destar en el oficio,
        soy de afuera.

– Prisons, Auschwitz, Buchenwald
Nicaragua.
To continue, today 4th July
the veteran (dispatched a whole load of blacks)
Military Attaché (Black Flag kills them in the air
    and kills them again on the floor)
will decorate
the heroic and gallant
    soldiers.
    Soropeta, Juan Pluma, El Dormido,
    Casachica – you went off and left me
    in prison
    condemned me
    like a thief –
Toro Nuevo, el Burrito, el Zopilote
Black Ace,
    Lollipop
Lollipop arrives
    La Caleta, in spite of the dust
this boy is the goods.
    – If you give me food you can bugger me
for three cigarettes I'll suck it.
Moon, lilies, God,
the apolitical poet!
– A turkey hen she passed this way
oh so dainty, oh so jaunty.
In her beak she carries flowers
and on her wings her dearest loves.
    – Yesterday I nicked a radio.
    Yes, I have been
    at it ten years.
    I am from abroad.

Apúrese tengo que ganar,
oiga los chavalos
        cómo lloran,
no han comido,
mañana vienen
a cobrar la pieza,
acabe rápido.
– Vigile a esos hombres
cuidado sacan un papelito.
Ya saben
        ojo y oído.
– Ayer hubo vergueo
en la montaña,
– hablá más bajo,
la cosa está pegando.
Vinieron unas jañas
pijuditas a visita,
no conocimos
a Managua en
        minifalda.

Hurry up I have to get on,
listen to the children
       crying,
they have not eaten,
tomorrow they are coming
for the rent,
be quick about it.
       Watch those men
be careful if they take out a paper.
They know
       eye and ear.
– Yesterday there was a cock-up
in the mountain,
– talk more quietly,
something's going on.
Some pretty girls came
sweetly to visit,
We missed
Managua in
       miniskirts.

CARLOS JOSÉ GUADAMUZ

UNA FLOR

En mi celda hay una flor.
La encontré en un rincón
sola y como castigada.
Brotó del duro piso
de cemento y piedra.
Rompió la prohibición
de nacer en una celda.
Ningún pájaro he visto entrar
a depositar la semilla.
Ninguno le hizo surco
       para echarla.
Ninguna gota de lluvia
para que reventara.
Nació así.
Sola, sin ayuda de nadie
en un rincón propicio.

La celda, con ella
       ya no es celda.
Ahora es jardín.
Jardín de una rosa.
Sola ella, solita.
Mi rosa encarcelada,
prisonera política.

Lunes 8 de julio de 1974

50

CARLOS JOSÉ GUADAMUZ

A FLOWER

In my cell there is a flower.
I found it standing in the corner
alone as if for punishment.
It sprouted through the floor
of hard cement and stone.
It broke the prohibition
and was born in a cell.
I saw no bird fly in
to drop the seed.
No one dug the earth
        to plant it.
Not a drop of rain
to water it.
It sprouted just like that.
By itself, with no one's help
in a corner that suited it.

Now the cell
        is a cell no longer.
It has become a garden.
A garden with one blossom.
Just one, all alone.
My imprisoned rose,
a political prisoner.

Monday 8th June 1974

LEONEL RUGAMA

LA TIERRA ES UN SATELITE
DE LA LUNA

El Apolo 2 costó más que el Apolo 1
el Apolo 1 costó bastante.

El Apolo 3 costó más que el Apolo 2
el Apolo 2 costó más que el Apolo 1
el Apolo 1 costó bastante.

El Apolo 4 costó más que el Apolo 3
el Apolo 3 costó más que el Apolo 2
el Apolo 2 costó más que el Apolo 1
el Apolo 1 costó bastante.

El apolo 8 costó un montón, pero no se sintió
porque los astronautas eran protestantes
y desde la luna leyeron la Biblia,
maravillando y alegrando a todos los cristianos
y a la venida el papa Paulo VI les dio la bendición.

El Apolo 9 costó más que todos juntos
junto con el Apolo 1 que costó bastante.

Los bisabuelos de la gente de Acahualinca tenían menos
        hambre que los abuelos.
Los bisabuelos se murieron de hambre.
Los abuelos de la gente de Acahualinca tenían menos
        hambre que los padres.
Los abuelos murieron de hambre.

LEONEL RUGAMA

THE EARTH IS A SATELLITE OF THE MOON

Apollo 2 cost more than Apollo 1
Apollo 1 cost enough.

Apollo 3 cost more than Apollo 2
Apollo 2 cost more than Apollo 1
Apollo 1 cost enough.

Apollo 4 cost more than Apollo 3
Apollo 3 cost more than Apollo 2
Apollo 2 cost more than Apollo 1
Apollo 1 cost enough.

Apollo 8 cost a bomb, but they did not mind
because the astronauts were protestants
and read the Bible from the moon,
amazing and delighting all christians
and when they came Pope Paul VI gave them a blessing.

Apollo 9 cost more than all of them put together
including Apollo 1 which cost enough.

The great grandparents of the Acahualinca people
      were less hungry than the grandparents.
The great grandparents died of hunger.
The grandparents of the Acahualinca people
      were less hungry than the parents.
The grandparents died of hunger.

Los padres de la gente de Acahualinca tenían menos
    hambre que los hijos de la gente de allí.
Los padres se murieron de hambre.
La gente de Acahualinca tiene menos
    hambre que los hijos de la gente de allí.
Los hijos de la gente de Acahualinca no nacen
    por hambre,
y tienen hambre de nacer,
    para morirse de hambre.
Bienaventurados los pobres porque de ellos será la luna.

1969

The parents of the Acahualinca people were less
    hungry than the people's children from there.
The parents died of hunger.
The Acahualinca people are less
    hungry than their children.
The children of the Acahualinca people are not born
    for hunger,
and they are hungry to be born,
    in order to die of hunger.
Blessed are the poor because theirs shall be the moon.

1969

LAS CASAS SE QUEDARON
LLENAS DE HUMO

A los héroes sandinistas:
   Julio Buitrago Urroz
   Alesio Blandón Juárez
   Marco Antonio Rivera Berríos
   Aníbal Castrillo Palma

Y vi los huecos que la tanqueta Sherman
   abrió en la casa del barrio Frixione.
            Y después fui a ver más huecos
            en otra casa por Santo Domingo.
Y donde no había huecos de Sherman
   había huecos de Garand
            o de Madzen
                     o de Browning
o quién sabe de qué.
Las casas quedaron llenas de humo
   y después de dos horas
            Genie sin megáfono gritaba
            que se rindieran.
Y antes hacía como dos horas
y antes hacía como cuatro horas
y hacía una hora
gritaba
      y gritaba
            y grita.
Que se rindieran.
Mientras la tanqueta
      y las ordenes.
Las Browning
      las Madzen

THE HOUSES REMAINED FULL OF SMOKE

To the Sandinista heroes:
  Julio Buitrago Urroz
  Alesio Blandón Juárez
  Marco Antonio Rivera Berríos
  Aníbal Castrillo Palma

I saw the holes made by the Sherman tank
    in the house in the Frixione district.
            And later I went to see more holes
            in another house in Santo Domingo.
And where there were no Sherman holes
        there were holes made by Garands
            Madzens
                or Brownings
or who knows what.
The houses remained full of smoke
        and after two hours
                Genie without a megaphone shouted
                at them to surrender.
And about two hours before
and about four hours before
and about an hour ago
he was shouting
        and shouting
                and keeps shouting
at them to surrender.
Meanwhile the tank
        and the orders.
The Brownings
        Madzens

las M-3
los M-1
y las carretas
las granadas
las bombas lacrimógenas...
y los temblores de los guardias.

NUNCA CONTESTO NADIE.
Porque los héroes nunca dijeron
que morían por la patria,
sino que murieron.

1969

    M-3s
        M-1s
and the trucks
grenades
    teargas bombs...
and the guards quaking.

NO ONE EVER ANSWERED.
Because the heroes never said
        they were dying for their country.
They just died.

1969

EPITAFIO

Leonel Rugama
gozó de la tierra prometida
en el mes más crudo de la siembra
sin más alternativa que la lucha,
muy cerca de la muerte,
pero no del final.

EPITAPH

Leonel Rugama
enjoyed the promised land
in the bleakest month of sowing
with no alternative but the struggle,
very close to death
but not to the end.

ME ES NECESARIO TU CUERPO

Lo que dices.
Lo que miras.
Lo que grita
la redondez de tu ombligo.
Lo que nombras.
Lo que ríes.
Lo que vida.
La posible magia de tus ojos
y todo lo que escondes con fervor tan íntimo
y todo lo que agitas mortal y combatiente
como espina dorsal residente vertical del viento.

En esta parte del tiempo y en esta parte del mundo
tengo que alumbrar tu cuerpo
con los materiales de esta nueva conciencia
en la espera de un sueño
y un acto de esperanza
y sin edad el universo
y el fuego creador de tu presencia
penetre y recorra e incendie la médula de mis huesos.

Que la vida, la alegría
y las promesas
sean con nosotros.

Ahora después de todo
la tierra tiene el corte de tu cuerpo
y en esto soy la voz que emigra en tus latidos

RICARDO MORALES AVILÉS

YOUR BODY IS NECESSARY TO ME

What you say.
What you look at.
What your round belly button
shouts.
What you tell.
What makes you laugh.
What is your life.
Your eyes' possible magic
and everything you hide with such intimate fervour
and everything you do, you who are mortal but resist
like the wind's resident backbone.

In this part of time and this part of the world
I am to light up your body
with this new awareness
our dream of the future,
an act of hope
for the ageless universe.
Then the fire in you
can seek and kindle the marrow of my bones.

Life and joy
and promises
be with us.

For after all
the earth has the cut of your body
and I am the voice muttering in your heartbeats

en testamento de todo mi destino.

Porque en ti he clavado la última palabra
de mi canto
y en tus ojos apunto profecías al infinito
y dilato cada gota de alegría.

Hay tanto de tus brazos
y tanto de tu rostro y tanto de tu ternura
como sustancia del universo
y tanto de mi sangre a través de tu piel
y tanta respiración tuya preñada de mis temblores
y tanta historia
y tanto más,
que hay dos formas
y es una vida
y por todos lados existes tú
y la lucha continúa.

entrusted with all my destiny.

On you I have hung
my song's last words
for in your eyes I glimpse infinite prophecies
and brim with every drop of your joy.

There is so much of your arms
so much of your face and so much of your tenderness
which is the substance of the universe
and so much of my blood through your skin
and so much of your breath pregnant with my trembling
and so much history
and so much more,
that we are two forms
and it is one life
and everywhere there you are
and the struggle continues.

DORIS MARIA, CAMARADA

Vengo camarada, con las manos llenas
del polvo de esta tierra, sobre los hombros
cargando los dolores de este pueblo.

Vengo hasta ti
con el alma sudando todo el odio
porque alguien inventó la esclavitud,
cogió su arma
y alguien más tuvo hambre y frío
y empezaron a morir nuestros hermanos,
nuestros padres y nuestros hijos.

Vengo cantando
y hay dolores trenzados con la piel de mi cuerpo.
Tú me comprendes, camarada,
porque también te pesan estos crepúsculos
que nos han echado encima.

Vengo jubiloso
para juntar a tu cruzada
la audacia de mi brazo fuerte.
La lucha está difícil. Y hay que seguir
adelante y cuesta. Cuesta arriba.
Todo el que anda derecho
tiene en su haber una sonrisa y una onza de plomo.
No hay otra manera de contar la historia.

El fusil para todos,
lágrimas, flores y recuerdos para todos.

DORIS MARIA, COMRADE

I come, comrade, with my hands full
of this land's dust, my shoulders
loaded with its people's sorrows.

I come to you
with my soul sweating hatred
because someone invented slavery,
grabbed their weapon,
and someone else was hungry and cold
and our brothers began to die
and our parents and children.

I come singing
though the skin of my body is shot through with pain.
You understand me, comrade,
because these evenings they have piled upon us
also weigh on you.

I come rejoicing
to offer my bold strong arm
to your crusade.
The struggle is hard. And we must keep going
on and up. Uphill.
All that walks straight
has a smile in its step, and an ounce of lead.
There is no other way to tell history.

Arms for all,
tears, flowers and memories for all.

Hay que seguir entonces,
la historia tiene un solo sentido.
Y hay siempre y cada vez nuevas espadas
y una vieja manera de levantar la frente.

Hay que cambiar tantas cosas, camarada.
Primero el poder, la propiedad, nosotros,
y después... aire fresco y maíz para todos,
aire y flores para todos,
ternura para calentar los pies desnudos,
una canción, una camisa,
luz para el camino,
manos para la producción y el amor,
campanas, palabras
para la sonrisa de los niños.
Hay que cambiar tantas cosas. Por esto
he venido. A pedirte que nos eches una mano.
Tanto como de ti se acumula en nuestro esfuerzo.
Por esto he venido. A seguir el trazo de tus
pies de tierra nueva, a iluminarme con
el ardor de la invención de tu palabra.

Tú has sabido de injusticias y te pusiste
a inventar la esperanza
y así se fue desparramando por todos
los rincones de la patria.
Has sabido de alegrías recortadas, de ultrajes,
persecución y prisiones...
tanto para confeccionar lecciones
y tu dolor se mezcla con el crepitar de nuestra sangre.
No he venido solo. No estamos solos.
Somos muchos, camarada. Somos millones.

Then we must go on,
history has only one meaning.
And there are always new weapons each time
and an old way of lifting the head.

There are so many things to be changed, comrade.
First power, property, ourselves,
and then... fresh air and maize for all,
air and flowers for all,
tenderness to warm bare feet,
a song, a shirt,
light for the road,
hands for production and love,
bells, words
for children's smiles.
There are so many things to be changed. This is what
I have come for. To ask you to lend us a hand.
There is so much of you in our effort.
This is what I have come for. To follow the print
of your new-earth footsteps. To be lit
by your words' fire and inventiveness.

You have known injustices
and you set about creating hope
and thus it began pouring
through every corner of the country.
You have known joys cut short, outrages,
persecution and prisons...
enough to give lessons
and your suffering roars in our blood.
I have not come alone. We are not alone.
We are many, comrade. We are millions.

Nuestro grito recorre la piedra vertebral
de nuestra América, piedra del mundo,
para juntarse después de la montaña.
Este país se levantó con el sol del mediodía
y le damos la bienvenida a la mañana guerrillera.

Somos millones, Doris María de Nicaragua,
muchacha combatiente del pueblo,
geografía de nuestros campos, de nuestras costas
y de nuestros ríos.
Somos millones y desde pequeños
estamos soñando
y la insistencia vuelve otra vez a retoñarnos.

Somos millones y tú eres bandera y escudo,
chispa y camino,
ejemplo y llave,
Doris María camarada.

Cárcel de La Aviación, 1970

Our cry runs down the rocky backbone
of our America, the world's stone skeleton,
and after that it goes on gathering.
This land rose with the midday sun
and we welcome the guerrilla morning.

We are millions, Doris Maria of Nicaragua,
the people's young woman combatant,
geography of our fields, our coasts
and our rivers.
We are millions and we have been dreaming
since we were little,
and now this persistence is making us sprout again.

We are millions and you are flag and shield,
spark and road,
example and key,
Doris Maria, comrade.

La Aviación Prison, 1970

CARTA A ANA JOSEFINA

Hoy en tu segundo cumpleaños
tu padre recuerda
el escalofrío
el momento de amor
en que decidió
junto a tu madre
traerte a la vida

Esto quiere decir
que no te anunciaron
las barajas
que no naciste por un error
de las manecillas
o por la impresión
del arrullo

No olvido el día
en que todo comenzó
tu madre y yo compartimos
en una noche tibia de agosto
la emoción
el tabernáculo
Estábamos seguros del milagro

Después
cuando te hiciste ola
dentro del cuerpo
de tu madre

TOMÁS BORGE

LETTER TO ANA JOSEFINA

Today on your second birthday
your father remembers
the shudder
the moment of love
when he and your mother
decided
to bring you to life

This means
you were not foretold
by the cards
you were not born
through an error of the clock
or through importunate
canoodling

I have not forgotten the day
it all began
your mother and I shared
the feeling
the tabernacle
on a warm August night
We were sure of the miracle

Afterwards
when you became
a wave
inside your mother's body

estuvimos alertas
para disfrutar
el susurro de tus manos

El día que naciste
– 12 de abril de 1975 –
quisieron asesinarme

Pero estaba tan protegido
con tu madera limpia
que no hubo lugar
para la muerte

Luego
caí preso
y los enemigos escribieron
cicatrices
en mis costillas
y en las fronteras
del alma

Encapuchado y esposado
miré
durante nueve meses
desde un escenario
de líquen
el desfile
de la tinieblas

Íngrimo
pero ya con el derecho
de cerrar los puños

we were alert
to enjoy
your whispering hands

The day you were born
– 12th of April 1975 –
they tried to assassinate me

But I was so protected
by your newness
there was no room
for death

Later
I was arrested
and enemies wrote
scars
on my ribs
and my soul's
frontiers

Hooded and handcuffed
for nine months
in a lichen-clad
cubby-hole
I watched
the procession
of darkness

In solitary
but now with the right
to clench my fists

me aferré a tu memoria
tuve necesidad de ser digno
hija mía
para merecerte

Si hubiera caído
de rodillas
te pediría
que renegaras de mí
Pero fui y seré leal
al catecismo
y a las herejías

Aunque sin mérito
– soy apenas
un grano de maíz –
anhelo que te sientas
orgullosa del hombre
que abrazó
a tu madre

Tu madre sí es un oasis
Ella lavaba
hasta el agotamiento
tus pañales clandestinos
Y vive como una antorcha
un tornillo
un lago de amapola

Yo estaré siempre
sediento de tu amor
pero tu madre

I clung to your memory
I needed to be worthy
of you my daughter
deserve you

If I had grovelled
on my knees
I would ask you
to write me off
But I was and will be
loyal to catechism
and heresies

Although without merit
– I am barely
a grain of maize –
I want you to feel
proud of the man
who embraced
your mother

Yes, your mother is an oasis
She washed
your clandestine nappies
to the point of exhaustion
And her life is a torch
a strong bolt
a lake of poppies

I will forever be
thirsty for your love
but your mother

deberá estar por encima
de todo
inédita
como una hostia

Ella se parece
a las tardes de Managua
durante el verano
al beso de las palomas que rastrean
las aguas dulces
de tantos mares interiores

No sé si moriré
cuando canten los gallos
de este próximo invierno
Mas si se enfrían mis manos
y desaparecen la malicia
y la ternura de mis ojos
seguiré viviendo

Seguiré
si sos generosa
si en tu corazón
no tiene cabida el egoismo
si te enfrentas
dulce y colérica
a las injusticias

must always
come first
special
as communion bread

She is like
those Managua evenings
in summer
like doves' kisses
skimming the fresh waters
of all those inland seas

I don't know if I'll die
when the cocks crow
this coming winter
But if my hands grow cold
and my eyes lose their teasing gleam
their tenderness
I shall live on

I shall go on
if you are generous
if in your heart
egoism finds no room
and with your sweetness and your rage
you stand firm
against injustices

Entonces
el momento en que tu madre y yo
fuimos un solo cuerpo
para iniciar tu vida
tendrá sentido
Se justificará la luz
que quisimos encender

Cárcel de Tipitapa, 12 de abril de 1977

Then
the moment when your mother and I
became a single body
to bring you into being
will make sense
The light we wanted to strike
will shine

Tipitapa Prison, 12th April 1977

VISITA A LA CARCEL

Como la sangre
o el perfil
de un gato

Como la riña
solidaria
del sol

Como la clorofila
en los cascos
de los caballos frescos

Quiero el paso
de tus sandalias de espuma
de tus sandalias de bronce

Tu boca lenta
y la descarada luna
de tus rodillas de arena

Tu cintura – ese dígito
esa amenaza
de trapecio y legumbre

Dame el agua
en la espalda
para acariciar

PRISON VISIT

Like blood
or a cat's
silhouette

Like the sun
scolding
in solidarity

Like chlorophyll
in fresh horses'
hooves

I long for the tread
of your seafoam sandals
your sandals of bronze

Your slow mouth
and the barefaced moons
of your sandy knees

Your waist – that digit
that threat
of trapeze and vegetable

Give me water
on my back
to caress me

Dame la risa
las manos
las palabras

Dame
la limpia
la dulce piedra

Cárcel de Tipitapa, mayo de 1978

Give me laughter
hands
words

Give me
the clean
sweet stone

Tipitapa Prison, May 1978

LO TUYO Y LO MIO

Lo tuyo es mi
lengua tuya

Lo mío es tu
palabra mía

Soy tu nave
sos mi río

Mi naranja es
mi pájaro tuyo

Tu azul es
tu baraja mía

Ah nuestros
adverbios

Son míos
son tuyos

1988

YOURS AND MINE

Yours is my
tongue of yours

Mine is your
word of mine

I am your boat
you are my river

My orange is
my bird of yours

Your blue is
your pack of cards of mine

Oh our
adverbs

They are mine
they are yours

1988

LUIS ENRIQUE MEJÍA GODOY

LA VENGANZA

Mi venganza personal será el derecho
de tus hijos a la escuela y a las flores.
Mi venganza personal será entregarte
este canto florecido sin temores.
Mi venganza personal será mostrarte
la bondad en los ojos de mi pueblo.
Implacable en el combate siempre ha sido
y el más firme y generoso en la victoria.

Mi venganza personal será decirte
buenos días sin mendigos en las calles.
Cuando en vez de encarcelarte te propongan
que sacuda la tristeza de tus ojos,
cuando vos aplicador de la tortura
ya no puedas levantar ni la mirada.
Mi venganza personal será entregarte
estas manos que una vez vos maltrataste
sin lograr que abandonaran la ternura.

LUIS ENRIQUE MEJÍA GODOY

REVENGE

My personal revenge will be your children's
right to schooling and to flowers.
My personal revenge will be this song
bursting for you with no more fears.
My personal revenge will be to make you see
the goodness in my people's eyes,
implacable in combat always
generous and firm in victory.

My personal revenge will be to greet you
'Good morning!' in streets with no beggars,
when instead of locking you inside
they say: 'Don't look so sad!'
When you, the torturer,
daren't lift your head.
My personal revenge will be to give you
these hands you once ill-treated
with all their tenderness intact.

DORA MARÍA TÉLLEZ

VIVIMOS APRESURADOS

Vivimos apresurados
por eso
no puedo escribir
que al quedarme en la casa
en las mañanas
sentía tu presencia
en el pliegue de las sábanas.
Tal vez podría recordar
aquella vez
que lloramos en la posta
pensando en Ocotal,
cuando salíamos juntos
a subir agua de la quebradita
cuando planificamos
aquella exploración;
cuando comenzamos
a conocer nuestras caricias
en la troja, donde don Teyo
llena de pulgas la troja
pero llena de amor.

O podría recordar más atrás
cuando te reconocí
y discutimos de boxeo,
de la división
de los compañeros;
esa tarde se nos terminaron los cigarros
pero no las palabras.

DORA MARIA TÉLLEZ

WE LIVE IN A HURRY

We live in a hurry
that is why
I cannot write
that when I stayed at home
in the mornings
I felt your presence
in the crumpled sheets.
Perhaps I might recall
that time
we cried at the guard post
thinking of Ocotal,
when we went out together
to draw water from the spring
when we planned
that exploration;
when we began
to discover our caresses
in the barn, at Don Teyo's
full of fleas that barn was
but also full of love.

Or I might remember further back
when I had met you again
and we discussed boxing,
the division
among the compañeros;
that afternoon we ran out of cigarettes
but not of words.

O cuando en San Fabián
nos tocó la ametralladora treinta
disparando y disparando.
      Puedo recordar más...
      Hoy debemos hacer un pequeño documento
y ya es noche.

6 de junio de 1978

Or when in San Fabián
it was our turn with the machine gun 30
firing and firing.
I can remember more...
Today we must make a small report
and it is already night.

6th June 1978

FELIPE PEÑA

DIA DE LA LIBERACION

Hoy 23 de agosto a las 8 y media de la mañana
vi el sol reluciente
dejé de sentir tufo a mierda y a orines
ya no me picarán los zancudos ni dormiré
    en el piso de cemento
hoy se quedan las moscas y los gusanos
    en los hoyos de La Bartolina,
ya no estará encendida la luz en toda la noche
y los sayules que no me dejaban dormir.
No me dirá el teniente que soy anti patria
y que no merezco ni el aire que respiro,
se quedan los guardias que me quisieron matar y vos
gente de mi pueblo te quedás
con las manos levantadas desde el parque
diciendo adiós con tus pañuelos.

FELIPE PEÑA

LIBERATION DAY

Today 23rd of August at 8.30 in the morning
I saw the sun shining
I no longer smelt the stench of shit and urine
now the mosquitoes won't keep biting me
and I won't have to sleep on the concrete floor
today the flies and worms remain
            in the holes of La Bartolina,
now the light won't stay on all night
and the midges that did not let me sleep.
The warder will not tell me I am unpatriotic
and I don't deserve even the air I breathe,
the guards who tried to kill me are still there and you
people from home are still there
waving from the park
and saying goodbye with your handkerchiefs.

SON LAS CINCO Y MEDIA

Felipe Peña

SON LAS CINCO Y MEDIA

Son las 5 y media de la tarde, el tiempo está sereno
no se oye el sonido de la avioneta
    que vigila la frontera
sólo el gurún gurún de los compañeros
    que hablan desde sus champas
y el canto de los pájaros en la montaña al atardecer
la gongolona, el guás
la perdiz que silba como persona perdida en los bosques
el choschós
los congos que cantan con con con
el pájaro carpintero picotea en un palo seco
y los monos que hacen gracias en los árboles frondosos
chillan y botan ramas secas.
Esta tarde más que las otras
    se han animado más los grillos
que cantan ri ri ri como si anunciaran la lluvia que
    empieza a caer
la montaña se ha oscurecido
    nosotros vamos a hacer la posta
los otros a dormir sin haber cenado.

IT IS HALF PAST FIVE

It is half past 5 in the afternoon, the weather is calm
we do not hear the sound of the little plane
    surveying the frontier
only the mumble mumble of the comrades
    chatting in their tents
and evening birdsong in the mountain
the *gongolona*, the squawker crow
the partridge that whistles like someone lost in the wood
the *choschós*
the congo monkeys who cry *cong cong cong*
the woodpecker pecking at a dry tree
and monkeys playing among the leafy branches
shrieking and throwing down dead twigs.
This afternoon more than ever
    the crickets have been lively
singing *ree ree ree* as if announcing rain
    beginning to fall
the mountain has grown dark
    we are going to stand guard
and the others to sleep without any supper.

UN BUEN DIRIGENTE

Te conocí a principios del mes de septiembre:
íbamos en una columna de 35 soldados del ejército
                              del pueblo;
vos ibas en la retaguardia con la compañera Marta y yo.
Tu pseudónimo era Martín.
Vos y El Danto comandaban la columna;
este último, experto en caminatas en las montañas
                              de Nicaragua,
iba adelante dirigiendo la marcha.
Estuvimos sentados descansando bajo la sombra de unos
                              árboles frondosos
que encontramos al subir una de las lomas.
Ibamos llegando cuando me gritó el Danto:
– Escóndanse que los ven los aviones.
Me sorprendió su voz
intenté correr y me caí.
Otro grupo de compañeros había hecho un pequeño
                              ataque al comando
de Peñas Blancas esa mañana
y la aviación estaba bombardeando.
Oíamos los rockets que se estrellaban a cuatrocientos
                              metros.
Dieron la orden de avanzar.
Yo estaba envuelto en un bejucal.
Salimos a unos potreros;
el monte nos tapaba hasta las rodillas
y los aviones pasaban cerca.
Yo grité enojado:
– Esto es un atentado, nos traen de lo boscoso
a esto que está limpio. Y vos Martín gritaste:

Felipe Peña

A GOOD LEADER

I met you at the beginning of the month of September
we were in a column of 35 soldiers of the
people's army;
you were in the rearguard with *compañera* Marta and me.
Your pseudonym was Martín.
You and El Danto were commanding the column;
the latter, an expert in tracking through the mountains
of Nicaragua,
was in front leading the march.
We were sitting down to rest under the shade of some
leafy trees
which we found at the top of one of the hills.
We were just arriving when Danto shouted at me:
– Hide, the planes can see you.
His voice startled me
I tried to run and fell over.
Another group of *compañeros* had made
a small attack
on the Peñas Blancas garrison that morning
and the air force was bombing.
We heard the rockets exploding four hundred yards
away.
The order was given to advance.
I was tangled in a liana.
We came out to some fields;
the scrub covered us up to our knees
and the planes were flying near.
I shouted angrily:
– This is murder, you are bringing us out of the wood
into this open country. And you, Martín shouted back:

– No tengan miedo,
cuando el avión pase cerca siéntense y no se muevan.
Corriendo y sentándonos llegamos a la quebrada.
Ahí te quitaste los zapatos y como veías el desespero
de nosotros, con toda tranquilidad dijiste:
– Si nos cae una bomba hasta ahí llegaremos
pero nadie se va a correr.
Estuvimos hasta las 4 de la tarde. A las seis íbamos
llegando a la casa que ordenaste tomáramos.
Yo me asusté y tímidamente te pregunté:
– ¿No le vamos a hacer nada a esta gente?
Y vos respondiste en tono afirmativo: – NO.
Allí compraste un cerdo y dos gallinas.
La noche estuvo lluviosa, nos ascostamos en los ranchos
donde dormían las gallinas.
El compañero Malicia temblaba de fiebre
y no teníamos cobijas.
La noche siguiente íbamos de regreso
descartada la posibilidad de atacar el comando de Rivas.
En la carretera te tomó preso un guardia civil
y te deportó a Panamá,
hasta que te volví a ver en el campamento
dirigiendo los ejercicios de las 5 a las 6 de la mañana.
Recuerdo que por vos no me mandaron a otro
                                        campamento.
Desde entonces no supe nada de tí
hasta que oí la noticia
que la guardia del tirano te había matado en un combate
con tu nombre de sacerdote Gaspar García Laviana.
Cuando te conocí no sabía que eras cura;
para mí eras un buen dirigiente
entregado en cuerpo y alma a la lucha del pueblo.

– Don't be afraid,
when the plane flies over, sit down and don't move.
Running and sitting we arrived at the stream.
There you took off your shoes and as you saw our
hopelessness, you said quite calmly:
– If a bomb falls on us we will get over there
but nobody is going to run away.
We stayed there until 4 in the afternoon. At six we were
arriving at the house you had ordered us to take.
I was frightened and timidly asked you:
– We aren't going to do anything to these people?
And you answered very firmly: – NO.
There you bought a pig and two hens.
The night was rainy, we lay down in the huts
where the hens were sleeping.
Compañero Malícia was shivering with a temperature
and we had no blankets.
The following night we went back
seeing it was not possible to attack the Rivas garrison.
A civil guard arrested you on the road
and deported you to Panama.
Later I saw you again in the camp
leading the exercises from five till six in the morning.
I remember it was through you that I was not sent
                                        to another camp.
After that I knew nothing about you
until I heard the news
that the tyrant's Guard had killed you in a battle
and your name as a priest Gaspar García Laviana.
When I met you I did not know you were a priest;
for me you were a good leader
committed body and soul to the people's struggle.

ERSNESTO CASTILLO

AUNQUE MI VIDA

Aunque mi vida no alcance
el día de la victoria,
no será en vano mi lucha,
pues en la alegría del pueblo
habrá un sentimiento de tristeza
revuelto con esperanza
y dirán entonces:
– Compañeros,
recordemos a aquellos
caídos en combate.
Entonces todos sabrán
que no fue un gesto inútil
el mío, el de muchos
que sabemos que aunque
no lo veamos nosotros,
está cerca el día.

EVEN THOUGH MY LIFE

Even though my life does not last
till the day of victory,
my struggle will not be in vain,
because in the people's joy
there will be a feeling of sadness
intermingled with hope,
and then they will say:
– Comrades,
let us remember those
who fell in combat.
Then everyone will know
it was not a useless gesture,
what I did, what many of us are doing
who know that even though
we may not see it
the day is near.

DONDE LOS DESCONOCIDOS

Donde los desconocidos
derramaron su sangre
ahí donde dejaron
un recuerdo
oloroso a pólvora,
ahí voy a comenzar
la construcción
de alegrías y esperanzas.
Ahí donde los guardias
incendiaron ranchos,
donde el avión destrozó
aldeas,
levantaremos escuelas,
cooperativas,
hospitales,
con los nombres de aquellos
que murieron sin verlas.

WHERE THE UNKNOWN

Where the unknown
have shed their blood,
where they have left
a dust-smelling
memory,
that's where I'll start
building hope and joy.
Where the guards
set fire to farms,
where the aeroplane bombed
villages,
we will put up schools,
co-operatives,
hospitals,
called by the names of those
who died without seeing them.

AMANECER

Ya están cantando los gallos.
    Ya ha cantado tu gallo comadre Natalia
        ya ha cantado el tuyo compadre Justo.
Levántense de sus tapescos, de sus petates.
Me parece que oigo los congos
    despiertos en la otra costa.
Podemos ya soplar un tizón –
            botar la bacinilla.
    Traigan un candil para vernos las caras.
Latió un perro en un rancho
    y respondió el de otro rancho.
Será hora de encender el fogón comadre Juana.
La oscurana es más oscura pero porque viene el día.
    Levántate Chico, levántate Pancho.
Hay un potro que montar,
    hay que canaletear un bote.
Los sueños nos tenían separados, en tijeras
tapescos y petates (cada uno con su sueño)
    pero el despertar nos reúne.
La noche ya se aleja seguida de sus ceguas y cadejos.
Vamos a ver el agua muy azul:
        ahorita no la vemos. – Y
esta tierra con sus frutales, que tampoco vemos.
Levántate Pancho Nicaragua, cogé el machete
hay mucha yerba mala que cortar
    cogé el machete y la guitarra.
Hubo una lechuza a medianoche
    y un tecolote a la una.

DAYBREAK

Now the cocks are crowing.
    Now your cock has crowed mother Natalia
    and so has yours father Justo.
Get up from your bunks and your sleeping mats.
I think I can hear the congo monkeys
    awake on the other coast.
Now we can blow on some kindling –
                empty the chamber pot.
    Bring a candle to see our faces.
A dog barked in one hut
    and another hut's dog barked back.
It will be time to light the stove mother Juana.
The dark is darker but because day is coming.
    Get up Chico, get up Pancho.
There is a foal to ride,
    a boat to paddle.
Dreams kept us separate, on bunks,
cots and mats (each with our dream)
    but waking reunites us.
Now night departs with its demons and monsters.
We shall see the water very blue:
              now we can't see it. – And
this earth with its fruit trees, which we cannot see either.
Get up Pancho Nicaragua, take your machete
there are plenty of weeds to slash
    take your machete and your guitar.
There was a screech owl at midnight
    and an eagle owl at one o'clock.

Luna no tuvo la noche ni lucero ninguno.
Bramaban tigres en esta isla
y contestaban los de la costa.
Ya se ha ido el pocoyo que dice: Jodido. Jodido.
Después el zanate clarinero cantará en la palmera,
      cantará: Compañero
          Compañera.
Delante de la luz va la sombra volando como un vampiro.
      Levántate vos, y vos, y vos.
(Ya están cantando los gallos.)
        ¡Buenos días les dé Dios!

The night was moonless without a single star.
Tigers roared on this island
    and those on the other coast answered.
Now the nightjar has gone which says: So sod it! Sod it!
Soon the grackle will sing in the palm tree,
        it will sing: *Compañero*
                    Compañera.
Darkness flies before the light like a vampire.
    Get up you, and you, and you.
(Now the cocks are crowing.)
        God give you good morning!

OFENSIVA FINAL

Fue como un viaje a la luna
con la complejidad y precisión de todos los detalles
contando con todo lo previsto
                    y también lo imprevisto.
Un viaje a la luna en el que el menor error
                    podía ser fatal.
'Aquí *Taller*!' – 'Aló *Asunción*!' – 'Aló *Milpa*!'

Taller era León, *Asunción* Masaya, *Milpa* Estelí.

Y la voz calmada de la chavala Dora María desde *Taller*
diciendo que los refuerzos del enemigo
                    los estaban rodeando
peligrosamente,
la voz cantarina y calmada,
        'Aquí *Taller*. ¿Me están escuchando?'
Y la voz de Rubén en Estelí.
                    La voz de Joaquín en *Oficina*.
Oficina era Managua.
Oficina no tendría municiones en dos diás más.
                    ('Cambio'.)
Instrucciones precisas, en clave, dónde sería el
                                aterrizaje...
Y Dora María:'No tenemos bien guardada la retaguardia.
                    Cambio.'
Voces serenas, calmas, entrecruzándose
                    en la frecuencia sandinista.
Y hubo un tiempo en que el equilibrio de las dos fuerzas
                                se mantenía
y mantenía y estaba siendo muy peligroso.

FINAL OFFENSIVE

It was like a trip to the moon
with all its precise and complicated details
taking into account all that was foreseen
                      and also what was not.
A trip to the moon in which the slightest mistake
                      could be fatal.
'Workshop calling!' – 'Hullo *Assumption*!' –
                      'Hullo *Maizefield*!'
Workshop was León, *Assumption* Masaya,
                      Maizefield Estelí.
And young Dora María's placid voice from *Workshop*
saying enemy reinforcements
                    were surrounding them
dangerously,
her calm singing voice:
                'Workshop calling! Can you hear me?'
Rubén's voice in Esteli.
                Joaquín's voice in *Office.*
Office was Managua.
Office would run out of ammunition in two days' time
                ('Over!')
Precise instructions in code where the landing
                    would be...
And Dora María: 'Our rearguard is not well covered.
                Over!'
Serene calm voices crossing back and forth
                on the Sandinista radio.
And there was a time when the two forces
                  were balancing,
balancing, and things were very dangerous.

Fue como un viaje a la luna. Y sin ningún error.
Muchísimos trabajando coordinados en el gran proyecto.
La luna era la tierra. El pedazo nuestro de la tierra.
Y llegamos.
Ya empieza, Rugama, a ser de los pobres;
la tierra está
(con su luna).

It was like a trip to the moon. And there was no mistake.
So many working together in the one great project.
The moon was the earth. Our bit of earth.
And we got there.
And now Rugama, it's beginning to belong to the poor;
the earth is
> (with its moon).

A ERNESTO CASTILLO MI SOBRINO

Recuerdo Ernesto cuando volviste
            de tu entrenamiento
y hablabas de armas 'lindísimas'
            que habías aprendido a manejar,
'...es linda mamá' le decías a tu mamá,
como quien habla de la belleza de una muchacha.
Después una bala de francotirador te dió en la cara
cuando saltabas a la calle en León
gritando, para animar a los de tu escuadra que te seguían:

            ¡PATRIA LIBRE O MORIR!

Poeta caído a los 20 años.
Estoy pensando en esto Ernesto
ahora que los niños son besados por los soldados
y hay un taller de poesía en la Policía
y el ejército de Alfabetización con su uniforme
            azul y gris
está regado por todo el país, y hay Reforma Agraria
y los niños vendeperiódicos y limpiabotas
            son llevados a jugar
y... bueno, de verdad que fueron lindísimas esas armas
            (y recuerdo el brillo de tus ojos
                        cuando lo decías).

114

TO ERNESTO CASTILLO MY NEPHEW

I remember Ernesto when you came back
from your training
and spoke about the 'wonderful' weapons
you had learned to use,
'...she's wonderful, mama,' you told your mother,
like someone speaking about a beautiful girl.
Later a sharpshooter hit you in the face
when you leapt into the street in León
encouraging your squad to follow by shouting:

A FREE COUNTRY OR DEATH!

Poet who fell aged 20.
I am thinking about this Ernesto
now that children are kissed by soldiers
and there is a poetry workshop in the Police Station
and the Literacy army in their blue and grey uniform
have spread all over the country,
and there is Land Reform
and the child paper-sellers and boot-cleaners
are taken to play
and... well, it's true those weapons were wonderful
(and I remember the shine in your eyes
when you said it).

REUNION DE GABINETE

Citados para una reunión de gabinete,
de antemano sabiendo que por una razón muy importante
pero no cuál.
Todos los ministros y directores de entes autónomos
        en la gran mesa.
Y era una cuestión grave:
La integración de un Comité de Emergencia Nacional
por el peligro de plaga del mosquito *Aedes Aegypti*.
Se cría especialmente en recipientes artificiales.
        Puede reconocerse por sus líneas plateadas
                en el tórax.
Es la hembra la que pica al ser humano.
Necesita la sangre para sus huevos
que deposita en cualquier recipiente con agua.
Hay que hacer la campaña preventiva en
floreros, envases, llantas viejas, barrilles,
canales del techo,
        la eliminación de objetos inservibles
           limpieza en los patios,
                fumigación terrestre y aérea.
Oscuro y pequeño
la enfermedad que transmite
        de alta mortalidad en la niñez,
           peligrosa en los ancianos.
Muy posible que ocurra un brote en Nicaragua.
        Recursos materiales. Financieros.
Una intensiva campaña de propaganda.
El aporte de todos los organismos: Salud,
Transporte, Educación, Fuerza Aérea...
La participación de los trabajadores, estudiantes...

CABINET MEETING

We are summoned to a cabinet meeting,
knowing in advance it is for a very important reason
but not what.
All the ministers and directors of autonomous bodies
            round the big table.
And it was a serious matter:
the setting up of a National Emergency Committee
for the danger of a plague of *Aedes Aegypti* mosquitoes.
They breed especially in artificial vessels.
They can be recognised by the silver lines
                        on their thorax.
It is the female that bites human beings.
She needs their blood for her eggs
which she deposits in any vessel containing water.
A preventive campaign must be mounted in
vases, bottles, old tyres, barrels,
roof gutters,
        get rid of unuseful objects
                keep patios clean,
                    air and ground fumigation.
Small and dark
they carry an infection
                with a high mortality rate among children
                and dangerous to the old.
Very possibly there will be an outbreak in Nicaragua.
            Material resources. Financial.
An intensive propaganda campaign.
Support from all departments: Health,
Transport, Education, Air Force...
Involvement of workers and students...

Y miro las caras serias en torno de la gran mesa
           donde hay cartapacios, ceniceros,
y pienso: qué curioso,
qué curioso. Es el amor:
       el gabinete reunido por el amor al prójimo.

And I look at the serious faces round the big table
            strewn with files, ashtrays,
and I think: how odd,
how very odd. It's love.
    The cabinet meeting for love of their neighbour.

WASLALA

Ahora todo es alegre en Waslala.
Waslala, lindo nombre.
(Antes el sólo nombre aterrorizaba.)
Ya no vienen más los campesinos vendados y amarrados.
El atardecer ya no trae gemidos desgarradores
sino sones de guitarra.
Sin aquellos seres que gritaban:
'Viva la guardia, abajo el pueblo.'
Han venido muchachas del Cuá muy contentas,
con flores en la cabeza.
Ya pasó la pesadilla: 'Waslala'.
Está alegre Waslala, la
capital del terror y la muerte
para los campesinos del norte.
Era la cabecera del plan integral contrainsurgente,
del cerco estratégico de aniquilamiento guerrillero.
La peor de las 'aldeas estratégicas'
de represión campesina.
Ya no están con perros pastor-alemán
para rastrear revolucionarios.
Este risueño rincón de la montaña
que fue lo más tenebroso de la noche de Nicaragua.
Mataban a todos en el rancho.
Quemaban vivos en el rancho.
Waslala ya sin bestias.
Estas tierras para el maíz eran mudos cementerios.
A veces enterradas familias enteras.
Ya Pancho está con el machete desyerbando el maizal.
Para irse a bañar al río no hay que pedir
permiso al cuartel.

WASLALA

Now everything is happy in Waslala.
Waslala, lovely name.
(Once even the name caused terror.)
Now the peasants no longer arrive roped and blindfold.
The afternoon no longer carries bloodcurdling howls
but guitar sounds.
No toadies now shout:
'Long live the guard, down with the people!'
Young women from Cuá have come very cheerfully,
with flowers in their hair.
Now the Waslala nightmare is over.
Waslala is happy,
that once was the capital of terror and death
for the peasants in the North.
Headquarters of the whole counter-insurgency plan,
the strategic fence to annihilate the guerrillas.
The worst of the 'strategic villages'
to repress the peasants.
Now they no longer have German shepherd dogs
to track down revolutionaries.
This pleasant mountain corner
that was the darkest in Nicaragua's night.
They killed everyone on the farm.
They burnt people alive on the farm.
Waslala now without those brutes.
These maize lands were silent cemeteries.
Sometimes whole families were buried.
Now Pancho is hoeing the maize field with his machete.
You don't have to ask permission at the barracks
to bathe in the river.

La escuela de Waslala tendrá maestros
          y no a los de la Seguridad.
Los soldados verde-olivo juegan con los niños.
     Los campos ya no son de concentración.
Ya no ruge el helicóptero sobre los cerros con campesinos,
volviendo a los minutos con solo tripulación
          Aquí traían   los de Dudú
                              los de Kubalí
                              los de Kuskawás
                              los de Wanawás
                              los de Zinica
                              los de Zapote.
Aquí fueron calabozos, fueron cárceles subterráneas,
fueron los fosos con hombres, mujeres, niños y ancianos.
El monte está ya sin las fieras con uniforme
                              de camuflaje.
Los campesinos que vienen de otro lado
                    duermen en el cuartel.
               Cinco años fue la noche.
Qué bella está esta mañana la montaña,
la montaña donde anduvieron entre los monos
                    tantos guerrilleros.
Frente al comando los niños corren como colibríes.
Frente al CDS las mujeres charlan entre flores
                    como tucanes.
Las banderas roji-negras paracen pájaros.
Qué bello el verde de los campos
               y el verde de los compas.
     Qué lindo resbala ahora el río Waslala.
          De pronto vino el día.
     El cafe será bueno este año.
Qué alegre está Waslala.

The Waslala school will have teachers
        and not Security personnel.
Now olive green soldiers play with the children.
The camps are not concentration camps.
The helicopter no longer roars over the hills
with peasants, to return minutes later with only the crew.
Here they brought   people from Dudú
        people from Kubalí
        people from Kuskawás
        people from Wanawás
        people from Zinica
        people from Zapote.
Here there were prisons, underground dungeons,
graves full of men, women, children and old people.
Now the mountain no longer has wild beasts
        in camouflage uniform.
The peasants who come from elsewhere
        sleep in the barracks.
        For five years it was night.
How beautiful the mountain is this morning,
the mountain where so many guerillas went about
        among the monkeys.
In front of the garrison children flit like humming birds.
In front of the Civil Defence women chat among flowers
        like toucans.
The red and black flags look like birds.
How beautiful the green country
        and the green *compas.*
Now how sweetly the River Waslala slips by.
        Suddenly day came.
The coffee will be good this year.
Happy is Waslala!

COMANDANTE DOS

Dora María Téllez
    de 22 años
menuda y pálida
de botas, boina negra
el uniforme de guardia
    muy holgado.

Tras la baranda
yo la miraba hablar a los muchachos.
Bajo la boina la nuca
    blanca
y el pelo recién cortado.

(Antes de salir nos abrazamos)

Dora María
la aguerrida muchacha
que hizo temblar de furia
el corazón del tirano.

COMANDANTE DOS

Dora María Téllez
       22 years old
slight and pale
in boots, black beret,
her Guard's uniform
       very baggy.

Behind the railings
I watched her talking to the lads.
Beneath the beret her white
       neck.
and new cut hair.

(Before we went out we hugged)

Dora María
girl and veteran
who made the tyrant's heart
tremble with fury.

50 VERSOS DE AMOR
Y UNA CONFESION NO REALIZADA
A ERNESTO CARDENAL

De haber conocido a Ernesto como aparece
en una foto amarillenta que Julio me mostró:
flaco, barbón, camisa a cuadros y pantalón de lino,
las manos en los bolsillos
y un aire general de desamparo,
me hubiera metido por él en la Rebelión de Abril.
Juntos, habríamos ido a espiar a Somoza
en la fiesta de la embajada yanki.

¿Quién sería su novia en esos días?
La Meche o la Adelita o tal vez Claudia,
Ileana o Myriam. Muchachas eternamente frescas
que sonríen desde viejas fotografías
traspapeladas en quién sabe qué gavetas.

Myriam sale de la iglesia con su vestido amarillo
entallándole el cuerpo moreno y grácil.
Ileana pasa distante
más lejana que la galaxia de Andrómeda;
la Adelita palidece al doblar la esquina
y encontrarse de pronto con él;
Claudia prefiere las fiestas y las carreras de caballos
a un epigrama de Ernesto.
Meche es la más misteriosa.

Conocí a Ernesto el el año '72, oficiando
en el altar de la ermita de Solentiname.
Ni me habló; apenas me concedió el perfil.

50 LINES OF LOVE
AND AN UNMET CONFESSION
TO ERNESTO CARDENAL

If I had known Ernesto as he appears
in a yellowing photo Julio showed me,
thin, bearded, check shirt, linen trousers,
hands in his pockets
and a general air of helplessness,
I would have joined the April Rebellion for him.
Together we would have gone to spy on Somoza
at the party at the Yankee embassy.

Who might his girlfriend be in those days?
Meche or Adelita or perhaps Claudia,
Ileana or Myriam. Eternally fresh-faced girls
smiling from old photographs
wrapped away in some drawer.

Myriam comes of out church, her yellow dress
sculpting her brown and graceful body.
Ileana passes in the distance
further off than the Andromeda galaxy.
Adelita goes pale as she turns the corner
and suddenly runs into him.
Claudia prefers parties and horse races
to an epigram by Ernesto.
Meche is the most mysterious.

I met Ernesto in the year '72, celebrating
at the altar in the Solentiname chapel.
He did not speak to me. He barely looked my way.

Es la fecha y no se acuerda siquiera
de haberme visto entonces.

Después de la Insurrección del '78 al fin reparó en mí.
Se apareció en la clandestina Radio Sandino
interesado en conocerme al saber que yo era poeta
                      y combatiente.
Ni en mis sueños más fantásticos imaginé
que el encuentro sucedería así:
Allí venía tranquilo, como que si nada,
caminando entre el monte recién llovido.
Entró al caramanchel y preguntó por mí.

¿Para qué preguntó? Ese encuentro fue decisivo.
Desde el principio me entendí con él casi tan bien
como en otros tiempos con mi abuelo.
Allí es que comienza una larga historia:
Cuatro años ayudándole a inventar el mundo,
organizando el Ministerio de Cultura
con el fervor y la fe de un niño
en la madrugada de su Primera Comunión.
Esos años fueron casi felices
        (como diría Mejía Sánchez).

Aunque a estas alturas
        lo conmueva todavía algún recuerdo,
usted jamás se conformó con ninguna:
ni con Claudia, ni con todas las otras que no menciono.
Como San Juan de la Cruz o Santa Teresita
(que no quería una muñeca
        sino todas la muñecas del mundo)
sólo estuvo conforme cuando poseyó todo,

He does not even remember
seeing me at that date.

After the '78 insurrection at last he came to me.
He appeared in the clandestine Radio Sandino
wanting to meet me because he had heard I was a poet
                        and combatant.
Not even in my wildest dreams did I imagine
the meeting would be like that.
He arrived quietly, with no fuss
walking through the rainy mountain.
He came into the booth and asked for me.

Why did he ask? That meeting was decisive.
From the beginning I got on with him
almost as well as I used to get on with my grandfather.
It was the start of a long story:
four years helping him invent the world,
organising the Ministry of Culture
with the fervour and faith of a child
on the morning of her first communion.
These years were almost happy
            (as Mejía Sanchez would say).

Although at these lofty heights
            you may still be stirred by some memory,
you never met your match with anyone,
not Claudia, or any of the others, whom I won't mention.
Like St John of the Cross or little St Teresa
(who wanted not just one doll
            but all the dolls in the world)
you were only satisfied when you got the lot.

Todito el Amor.

Ahora posee a Dios a través del pueblo:
  ¡Esposo de Dios!
Por eso cuando le digo que de haber sido yo su novia
en ese entonces sus versos para mí
  no habrían sido en vano,
él me contesta: 'Qué lástima, no nos ayudó el tiempo.'
  Pero yo ni caso le hago.

Love as a whole.

Now he possesses God through the people.
        Wedded to God!
So when I tell him that if I had been his girlfriend
at that time his poems for me
        would not have been in vain,
he answers me: 'What a pity time was not on our side.'
        But I take no notice.

LUIS ROCHA

CONTRALUZ

El rostro moreno
de la muchacha
entre absorto e iluminado
sus ojos negros encendidos
el cabello sujeto a la tibia nuca
por un pañuelo rojinegro
del compa que la acompaña
que la ciñe de la cintura
mientras caminan y se observan
el perfil de ambos
acercándose
la tarde cayendo enamorada
sobre una calle de tierra limpia
bordeada de casas humildes
los labios
ya casi juntos
dejando pasar
sólo un destello de luz
antes del beso
después del triunfo
de la revolución.

Agosto de 1979

LUIS ROCHA

AGAINST THE LIGHT

The girl's dark face
absorbed, shining
her black eyes sparkle
her hair caught at the nape of her warm neck
by a red and black scarf
belonging to the *compa* who accompanies her
clasping her waist
as they walk, gazing
at one another
the profile of each
coming closer
the afternoon falling in love
along a clean earth street
bordered by modest houses
their lips
now nearly touching
with only a gleam
of light between them
before their kiss
after the triumph
of the revolution.

August 1979

133

NO VOLVERA EL PASADO

No volverá el pasado

Ya todo es de otro modo
Todo de otra manera
Ni siquiera lo que era es ya como era
Ya nada de lo que es será lo que era
Ya es otra cosa todo
Es otro era

Es el comienzo de una nueva era
Es el principio de una nueva historia
La vieja historia se acabó, ya no puede volver
Esta, ya es otra historia

Otra historia distinta de la historia
Otra historia contraria a la historia
Precisamente lo contrario de la historia
Precisamente lo contrario del pasado

No volverá el pasado

Precisamente es el pasado lo vencido
Precisamente es el pasado lo abolido
Precisamente es el pasado lo acabado
Ya el pasado realmente ha pasado

Ya el pasado realmente es pasado
El presente presente el futuro futuro

JOSÉ CORONEL URTECHO

THE PAST WILL NOT RETURN

The past will not return

Now everything is otherwise
Everything another way
Not even what was is now as it was
Now nothing of what is will be what it was
Now everything is something else
It is another era

It is the beginning of a new era
It is the beginning of a new history
The old history is over, now it cannot return
This is now another history

Another history different from the history
Another history contrary to the history
Precisely the contrary of the history
Precisely the contrary of the past

The past will not return

Precisely the past is what is beaten
Precisely the past is what is overthrown
Precisely the past is what is over and done
Now the past has really passed

Now the past is really past
The present present the future future

Antes era el pasado el presente el presente el pasado
Era imposible separar el presente del pasado
El pasado el presente el futuro eran sólo el pasado
Pero el pasado ya ha cambiado aun de significado
Todo el pasado ha sido juzgado y condenado
No volverá el pasado

Aun la misma palabra pasado tiene ya otro sentido
Y lo mismo la historia y la palabra historia
Porque la historia no era ya sino pasado
Historia ya estancada, fosilizada
Desde 1936 estaba detenida, empantanada
Era ya historia muerta, historia sin historia
Historia en la que el pueblo no contaba
Pero la historia es ya otra historia, nueva historia
Puesta de nuevo en marcha por el Frente
Puesta de nuevo en marcha por el pueblo
Ya es sólo historia lo que el pueblo quiera
Ya es sólo historia lo que el pueblo diga
Ya es sólo historia lo que el pueblo haga
La historia ahora cambiará de nombre
Tal vez se llame simplemente pueblo
Tal vez se llame simplemente vida
Tal vez Revolución, Verdad, Justicia
Tal vez se llame sólo Nicaragua

No hay ya palabra que no tenga otro significado
Ya las palabras tienen significado verdadero
Quiero decir, ya tienen verdadero significado
Quiero decir que ya significado quiere decir significado
No otra cosa distinta y mucho menos lo contrario
Lo que debe decir, no lo que quiere callar or falsear

Before the past was the present the present the past
It was impossible to separate the present from the past
Past present and future were only the past
But now the past has even changed its meaning
All the past has been judged and condemned
The past will not return

Even the very word past now has another meaning
Likewise history and the word history
Because history was nothing but the past
History stagnant, fossilised
Since 1936 it had been stopped, blocked
It was dead history, history with no story
History in which the people did not count
But now history is another story, a new story
Set in motion again by the *Frente*
Set in motion again by the people
Now history is only what the people want
Now history is only what the people say
Now history is only what the people do
Now history will change its name
Perhaps it may simply be called people
Perhaps it may simply be called life
Perhaps Revolution, Truth, Justice
Perhaps it may be called just Nicaragua

Now there is no word that has not got another meaning
Now words have true meaning
I mean, now they truly have meaning
I mean that now meaning means meaning
Not something different, much less the opposite
What it should say, not what it wants to deny or falsify

No lo que quiere disimular or simular
Sino sencillamente lo que quiere decir
La lengua estaba ya del todo corrompida
Una lengua que no servía más que para mentir
Una lengua que era a la vez mal español y mal inglés
No la lengua nicaragüense que habla el nicaragüense
Sino sólo un galimatías confeccionado para engañar
y robar y matar y mantenerse en el poder
Una angloalgarabía comercial para explotar
                                      al pueblo consumidor
Y sobre todo un modo de convertir en dólares el sudor
                                      del pueblo trabajador

Pero la lengua como todo lo que te fue robado
Como todo lo que te fue robado en el pasado
Todo ha sido por fin recuperado
Sólo de ti depende que sea tuyo ahora
Ya verás que tu lengua va a renacer purificada
Cada palabra ha sido pasada por el fuego,
                                      tratada en el crisol
Cada palabra tiene de nuevo sentido
El sentido de cada palabra, su propio sentido
Con el que fue inventada y acuñada,
                                      puesta en circulación
Aun su sentido original es ya un sentido nuevo
El sinsentido mismo tiene ya sentido
Como diría Joaquín Pasos, en el sentido de sentido
                                      y de sentido
Porque si no es sentido no es sentido
Si no se siente no es sentido
Es, pues, por tí, por vos, por todos,
Que por primera vez en Nicaragua

Not what it wants to dissemble or simulate
But simply what it wants to say
The language was wholly corrupt
A language that served only for lying
A language that was both bad Spanish and bad English
Not the Nicaraguan language spoken by Nicaraguans
Just a rigmarole concocted to trick
and rob and kill and keep itself in power
A commercial Anglo-gibberish to exploit
                               the consuming people
And above all a way of converting to dollars the sweat
                               of the working people
But language like everything else
                               of which you were robbed
Like everything you were robbed of in the past
All have at last been recovered
Now it is entirely up to you to make it yours
Now you will see your language reborn purified
Each word has been passed through the fire,
                               tried in the crucible
Each word again has sense
The sense of each word, its own sense
With which it was invented, nursed,
                               put into circulation
Even its original sense is now a new sense
Now nonsense itself has sense
As Joaquín Pasos would say, in the sense of sense
                               and sensed
Because if it is not sensed it is not sense
If you do not sense it it is not sense
So it is through you, through you, through all
That for the first time in Nicaragua

Todo es sentido
Es con sentido, consentido
Todo tiene sentido
La verdad ya es verdad
La mentira mentira
La patria patria
Y Nicaragua Nicaragua
La libertad por vez primera es libertad

Ya las palabras pronto serán ellas mismas
Ya pronto serán lo mismo las cosas y las palabras
Pronto será la misma cosa la palabra y la cosa
Como serán lo mismo las palabras y las obras
Como decía Santa Teresa: sus palabras son obras
Pronto vendrá la clarificación de las ideas
La redefinición de las palabras
La redefinición de la palabra revolución
La redefinición de la palabra democracia
La redefinción de la palabra sandinista
(Sandinista quiere decir nacional
                              — ha definido Tomás Borge
Sandinista quiere decir nicaragüense
                              — ha definido Tomás Borge)
Y la Revolución va a definir lo que es nicaragüense
Como el pueblo va a definir lo que es revolución
Como ha pasado ya el pasado y viene ya el futuro
                              por la Revolución
Como de ahora en adelante todo será
                              por obra de la Revolución
Como por la Revolución es que ya todo
                              es por primera vez
Es por primera vez en Nicaragua que una revolución

Everything is sense
It is with-sense, con-sent
Everything has sense
Now truth is truth
Lying is lying
Country country
And Nicaragua Nicaragua
For the first time freedom is freedom

Soon now words will be themselves
Soon now things and words will be the same
Soon the word and the thing will be the same thing
Just as words and works will be the same
As Saint Teresa said: their words are works
Soon will come the clarification of ideas
The redefinition of words
The redefinition of the word revolution
The redefinition of the word democracy
The redefinition of the word sandinista
(Sandinista means national
                    – in the definition of Tomás Borge
Sandinista means Nicaraguan
                    – in the definition of Tomás Borge)
And the Revolution will define what is Nicaraguan
As the people will define what is revolution
As now the past has passed and the future is coming
                    through the Revolution
As from now on everything will be
                    through the Revolution
As it is through the Revolution that now everything
                    is for the first time
It is for the first time in Nicaragua that a revolution

es la Revolución
La primera revolución contra todo el pasado
La primera que en realidad lo ha derrotado
La que de viaje lo ha borrado del mapa de Nicaragua
Hasta dejarlo todo en blanco o mejor dicho, en negro
Un agujero negro, un hueco negro, un hoyo negro,
                              como los hay en las galaxias
Eso es lo que ha quedado de todo el pasado
Por lo que solamente los del pasado viven en el pasado
Unicamente los del pasado añoran el pasado
Pero no se equivoquen.
                    Ya nadie en Nicaragua será engañado
No volverá el pasado.

is the Revolution
The first revolution against all the past
The first that has really defeated it
The one that has really wiped it off the map of Nicaragua
Leaving it white, or rather, black
A black void, a black hollow, a black hole
                    like the ones in the galaxies
This is what has remained of all the past
Because only those belonging to the past live in the past
Only those belonging to the past miss the past
But don't be mistaken.
              Now no one in Nicaragua will be abused
The past will not return.

A JUAN ACOSTA,
UN COMBATIENTE SOLITARIO

Granada 1979

Me contaron tu decisión de quedarte solo,
sin mi madre y mis hermanos para la Ofensiva Final
y que te dejaron dinero para que subsistieras.
Después me contaron que te habías vuelto loco:
– 'Imagínate,' me decían, 'gastarse
toda la plata en quintales de sal,
en vez de comprar alimentos.
Tiene la casa llena de sacos de sal.'
Pero yo, tu hija loca tan loca como vos,
me dije: 'Es la mejor inversión que ha hecho.'
Yo sabía para qué guardabas esa sal.
Te imagino entonces oyendo la clandestina
                              Radio Sandino
esperando la señal, espectante, siguiendo
diario la insurreción de Masaya,
seguramente casi escuchabas los tiroteos de León,
los bombardeos de Estelí, los combates
de los barrios orientales de Managua.
Descansabas en el día, para que el llamado
no te agarrara dormido.
                    En vano esperaste
el Atabal con su toque de guerra,
convocando a todo el pueblo a la insurreción.
Ni siquiera la Lucila vende-atol
gritó, llamó a la ciudad a la pelea.

LUZ MARINA ACOSTA

TO JUAN ACOSTA,
A SOLITARY COMBATANT

Granada 1979

They told me of your decision to remain alone,
without my mother or my brothers and sisters
                              for the Final Offensive
and that they left you money to live on.
Afterwards they told me you had gone crazy:
– 'Imagine,' they said, 'spending
all his cash on hundredweights of salt,
instead of buying food.
He's got the house crammed with sackfuls of salt.'
But I, your daughter am as crazy as you,
I said to myself: 'It's the best investment he ever made.'
I know what you were keeping that salt for.
I imagine you listening to the clandestine Radio Sandino,
expecting the signal, keeping track
of the insurrection in Masaya day by day.
Surely you could almost hear the firing in León,
the bombing in Estelí, the fighting
in the eastern districts of Managua.
You rested in the daytime so that the call
would not find you asleep.
                    You waited in vain
for the kettle drum with its war rattle
summoning the people to rise.
Not even Lucila the cold drink seller
crying the streets called the city to fight.

Ningún vecino te dijo cagado: 'Don Juan ya están aquí.'

Sólo vos estabas solo en Granada,
entre tus quintales de sal,
con tus sacos de sal, listo
para levantar la barricada de tu calle.
La sal solo sirvió para manchar los ladrillos de tu casa.
La Revolución triunfó sin necesitar de Granada,
pero vos, Juan Acosta, como un solitario soldado
                              del Frente Sandinista,
dispuesto, en la espera de tu combate, cumpliste.

Diciembre de 1981

No aghast neighbour told you: 'Don Juan they are here!'

Only you were alone in Granada
among your hundredweights of salt,
with your sackfuls of salt, prepared
to build your street's barricade.
The salt only stained the tiles in your house.
The Revolution triumphed without needing Granada,
but you, Juan Acosta, solitary soldier
of the Sandinista Front,
ready, waiting for your battle, did your bit.

December 1981

COMO ESCRIBIR UN POEMA DE AMOR

¿Cómo escribirte un poema de amor en la oficina?
Si las cartas que leo me entristecen:
Alfredo Matute, ciego de nacimiento,
solicita una guitarra
          y no tenemos.
Si a Marta Castillo le dijeron
que Ernesto Cardenal es director
          de un colegio de ballet.
Si Juan F. Delgado, coordinador
del CDS de 'El Limón',
escribe para que nos demos cuenta
de la pobreza de su comunidad.
Si no le entiendo a la letra de Jonás Bermúdez.
Si al Compañero Ministro
lo cuestionan por los Talleres de Poesía de campesinos
          y obreros.
Si las cuentas del teléfono son altas
          y no hay presupuesto.
Si ahora el chilamate ya no es aquella cúpula
de hojas y ya no me abraza con sus ramas
y la grama está amarilla de tan seca.
Si me dan asco los limpios, blancos inodoros
y los baños fríos de esta casa que fue de Somoza.
Tal vez cuando llegue a la casa
          te escriba un poema de amor.
Tal vez estas líneas son un poema de amor.

Enero de 1982

HOW CAN I WRITE A LOVE POEM?

How can I write you a love poem in the office?
If the letters I read make me sad:
Alfredo Matute, born blind,
asks for a guitar
        and we haven't got one.
If they told Marta Castillo
that Ernesto Cardenal is the director
        of a ballet school.
If Juan F. Delgado, co-ordinator
of the 'El Limón' Civil Defence,
writes to tell us about the poverty
of his people there.
If I cannot even read Jonás Bermúdez' writing.
If they keep asking the Comrade Minister
about the Poetry Workshops for peasants
        and workers.
If the telephone bills are high
        and there is no funding.
If the laurel-leafed fig tree is no longer that green dome
of leaves enfolding me in its branches
and the grass has turned yellow as it is so dry.
If I am nauseated by the clean, white lavatories
and cold bathrooms in this house that was Somoza's.
Perhaps when I get home
        I'll write you a love poem.
Perhaps these lines are a love poem.

January 1982

149

DAVID MACFIELD

CUANDO LLUEVE

Cuando llueve
el agua dice chis chis
las ranas cantan croac croac.

Mi mujer no canta
pero me encanta
cuando me toca
como quien toca una flauta
y me dice:
– '¡Ay acostémonos ya, amor!
que tengo frío.'

DAVID MACFIELD

WHEN IT RAINS

When it rains
the water says *chis chis*
the frogs chant *croac croac*.

My wife does not chant
but she enchants me
when she touches me
like a flute-player
and says:
– 'Oh, let's go to bed now, love!
I feel cold.'

BOSCO CENTENO

QUISE CONTARTE

Quise contarte cómo el río tiene
en su música una armonía de chorchas,
correas y martín-peñas, grillos y ranas,
de los saltos de los sábalos reales
en los remansos del río;
y de cómo las gallinitas de playa se
confunden con el violeta de las flores
de los gamalotes; pero vos despreciaste
mis poemas y te alejaste silenciosa
como el vuelo de una garza al atardecer.

BOSCO CENTENO

I WANTED TO TELL YOU

I wanted to tell you how the river has
a harmony of woodcocks in its music,
curlews and kingfishers, crickets and frogs,
how the great shad fish are leaping
in its backwaters;
and how the little hens on the beach
shade into the violet
of the flowering grasses, but you despised
my poems and went off without saying anything
like a heron flying at dusk.

A ELVIS CHAVARRIA

No vamos a recordarte con tu guitarra
en las noches de luna, poniendo serenatas
en las islas vecinas.
Ni con tu agilidad poco común en los deportes,
ni pescando con tu vara de madroño
en la Isla del Padre,
ni cazando iguanas a certeras pedradas.
Te vamos a recordar, hermano,
en la risa de los hijos de Oscar, de Pocho, de la Chica,
que corren y ríen sanos
por los rastrojos de las patria.

TO ELVIS CHAVARRIA

We are not going to remember you with your guitar
on moonlit nights, serenading
the neighbouring islands.
Or your uncommon agility at sports,
or fishing with your arbutus rod
on the Father's Island,
or hunting iguanas with well-aimed stones.
We will remember you, brother,
in the laughter of Oscar, Pocho and Chica's children,
who are laughing and running about
healthy all over the country.

OLGA APARICIA

Olga Aparicia es menudita en sus siete años
y ágil como una güisita.
A las seis y cuarenticinco, solita se levanta
y se prepara para irse a la escuela,
para regresar al medio día, alegrando la casa
                              con sus risas
y sus juegos interrumpidos con toda
seriedad para hacer sus tareas; y en la tardecita
a la Asociación de Niños Sandinistas
                              y regresa
hablando de Carlos Fonseca de Luis Alfonso y del Che;
se duerme a las ocho y al día siguiente comienza
                              otra vez;
y será, dice, poeta como su papá
                    y como su mamá pintora,
y revolucionaria como los dos.

OLGA APARICIA

Olga Aparicia is tiny at seven years old
and agile as a little flycatcher.
At six forty-five, she gets up all by herself
and gets ready to go to school,
to come back at midday, cheering the house
                                    with her laughter
and games, interrupted in all
seriousness to do her jobs; and in the afternoon
to the Association of Sandinista Children
                                    and she comes home
talking about Carlos Fonseca, Luis Alfonso and Che;
she goes to sleep at eight and next day begins
                                    all over again;
and she will be, she says, a poet like her dad
                                    and like her mum a painter,
and a revolutionary like them both.

A CHICHA (TONY),
CAIDO EN NUEVA GUINEA

Decías que para vos la muerte era
como un bello poema;
y cuando caíste tu sangre regó las mazorcas de maíz
que llevabas en los bolsillos del uniforme,
y sobre tu cuerpo puyonearon los granos
y crecieron grandes y fuertes espigas.

TO CHICHA (TONY),
WHO FELL IN NUEVA GUINEA

You said that for you death was
like a beautiful poem;
and when you fell your blood watered the maize cobs
you were carrying in your uniform pockets,
and on your body the grains sprouted
and grew to big strong shoots.

IVÁN GUEVARA

NO HAS VUELTO A LA BASE

Siempre amanece con el ruido de los pájaros cantando.
El día viene normal;
ruido de los camiones que entran y salen de la Base
donde trabajo.
Y por casualidad llegaste a la Base,
fue en aquel tiempos cuando Estados Unidos
había cortado el envío de harina a Nicaragua
y dejaste de trabajar en la panadería
y te vi contando caramelos por largo tiempo
en la Base.
Hablamos. Y tus ojos azules
también me miraron cariñosos
contentos de verme.

Y ahora que ha llegado la harina
no volviste a la Base,
y yo te he estado esperando
como el conejo que estuve esperando anoche
desde el torreón
y tampoco el conejo volvió a salir.
Sólo las urracas pasan por aquí de vez en cuando
y el viento tampoco ha soplado;
como cuando vienen las muchachas a bailar folclor
y el viento, antipático para ellas, levanta sus vestidos,
dejando ver sus blancas piernas.

IVÁN GUEVARA

YOU DIDN'T COME BACK TO THE CAMP

Dawn always breaks to the sound of birdsong.
A normal day:
sound of lorries coming in and leaving the Camp
where I work.
And you happened to come to the Camp,
it was that time when the United States had cut off
the supply of flour to Nicaragua
and you stopped working in the baker's
and I saw you counting sweets for a long time
at the Camp.
We talked. And your blue eyes
looked at me kindly
pleased to see me.

And now the flour has arrived
you have not come back to the Camp,
and I have been waiting for you
like the rabbit I was waiting for last night
from the watch tower
and the rabbit did not come out again either.
Only occasional magpies pass here
and neither did the wind blow:
as when the girls come to do folkdancing
and the wind, which they dislike, lifts their dresses,
showing their white legs.

MARTHA BLANDINO

NARCISO

Llegué a tu rancho de paja y bambú
en Los Pocitos, Narciso.
Las seis de la tarde,
y prendí la lámpara Coleman
porque en la montaña oscurece temprano.
Cansada, llena de inquietudes;
concocer cómo vivís vos y tus vecinos,
saber si cumpliría mi compromiso;
también unirme a tu pobreza
aguantar hasta el final de la Cruzada.
Narciso, ahora,
terminada la Campaña
entre la nostalgia de dejarlos
y la alegría de venirme
siento la satisfacción de saber
que, juntos,
hemos aprendido a conocer más este proceso.

MARTHA BLANDINO

NARCISO

Narciso, I arrived at your hut made of straw and bamboo
in Los Pocitos.
It was six in the evening
and I took the Coleman lantern
because it gets dark early in the mountains.
I was tired and anxious.
How did you and your neighbours live?
Would I manage to do my job?
What would it be like sharing your poverty?
Could I last out till the Crusade's end ?
Narciso, now
the campaign is over
I feel sad to be leaving you,
happy to be going home
and satisfied knowing
that, together, we have both
learnt a lot about this whole process.

LESBIA RODRÍGUEZ

POEMA A UN CEDECISTA

Fue una noche de invierno
que nos conocimos
               íntimamente.
Me preguntaste si sentí frío.
En ese momento
sentí acercarte poco a poco a mi cama.
Tu cercanía aceleró mi corazón.
Tu cuerpo
se fue juntando al mío
hasta quedar en un solo cuerpo.
De lo que no me arrepiento.

LESBIA RODRÍGUEZ

POEM TO A CIVIL DEFENCE MEMBER

It was a winter night
when we got to know each other
          intimately.
You asked me if I felt cold.
At that moment
I heard you creeping little by little towards my bed.
Your nearness made my heart beat faster.
Your body
was joining with mine
until we became just one body.
And I don't regret it.

Lesbia Rodríguez

REFLEXION DESPUES DE LEER UN POEMA

'Mañana, hijo mío,
todo será distinto.'
Edwin Castro

Todo es distinto.
Los parques llenos de niños riendo.
Los padres de la mano con sus hijos.
Y vos hijo, que todavía estás en mi vientre,
acariciándote con mis manos en la panza
y platicando con vos del futuro,
del Parque Luis Alfonso, Las Piedrecitas etc.,
donde te llevaré a jugar con los mimados
                    de la ANS y Los Carlitos.
Y te cuidaré como cuidan nuestros soldados
                    a la Revolución.
Y crecerás y multiplicarás la tierra con tus hijos.
Y yo sea más vieja
y Nicaragua más joven.

REFLECTION UPON
READING A POEM

'Tomorrow, my child,
everything will be different.'
Edwin Castro

Everything is different.
The parks full of children laughing.
Parents holding their children by the hand.
And you, child, who are still in my womb,
I stroke you with my hands brushing my belly
and talk to you about the future,
the Luis Alfonso Park, Las Piedrecitas, etc.,
where I will take you to play with the cosseted tots
in the ANS and Los Carlitos.
And I will take care of you as our soldiers take care
of the Revolution.
And you will grow and fill the land with your children.
And I will be older
and Nicaragua younger.

JOSÉ MENDOZA

A UN POETA
QUE NO LE GUSTA LA POESIA

Un técnico cubano de nombre Roque
me dice que no le gusta la poesía.
A él que está fuera de su patria,
lejos del hijo, lejos de aquello
que hace de su vida: risa y llanto
en su bella isla,
                              a él
cumplido en cada tarea,
que se levanta a las 6 a.m.
para estar más temprano en su trabajo
no le gusta la poesía.
Sin embargo él es poeta sin darse cuenta.
Está haciendo un bello poema del hombre,
curando las heridas abiertas
como lo hace un verdadero poeta.

JOSÉ MENDOZA

TO A POET
WHO DOES NOT LIKE POETRY

A Cuban technician whose name is Roque
tells me he doesn't like poetry.
He who is away from home,
far from his child, far from
his own life: laughter and sadness
on his beautiful island,
                    he
who takes such trouble with every job,
gets up at six a.m.
to be at work early
does not like poetry.
Nevertheless he is a poet unawares.
He is making a fine poem of human beings,
curing open wounds
as a true poet does.

JUAN RAMÓN FALCÓN

LORENA FABER 'LINDA'

Cuando llegó al campamento
con un *blue-jeans* (lee) desteñido
y una camisa de varón a cuadros
no había armas: un palo le sirvió
                    en los entrenamientos.
(En el campamento siempre pareció más bella
                    de lo que era.)
Días después con un Winchester 22 tiro a tiro
se quedaba haciendo posta
acompañada de Juan o de Tito.
A los dos meses su *blue-jeans* estaba lleno de FSLN
          (fue cuando le dieron su primer verde-olivo).
En esos días fue trasladada a Estelí.
Yo la ví una vez en la ciudad
                    (nadie sospechó de ella)
sus quince años la hacían verse más niña
                    que guerrillera.
Me contó todo esto y me regaló
este pañuelo rojo y negro
que es lo único que guardo de ella
y eso es todo lo que puedo decirte Mayra
porque después que la agarró la guardia
no volví a saber nada de Lorena.

JUAN RAMÓN FALCÓN

LORENA FABER 'LINDA'

When she arrived at the camp
in faded (Lee) blue jeans
and a man's check shirt
there were no weapons: she had to make do with a stick
            in the training exercises.
(In the camp she always looked more beautiful
            than she was.)
Days later with a Winchester 22 she stood guard
together with Juan or Tito.
After two months her blue jeans had FSLN written
            all over them
      (it was then they gave here her first olive green).
In those days she was transferred to Estelí.
I saw her once in the city
            (nobody suspected her)
her fifteen years made her look more like a child
            than a *guerrillera*.
She told me all this and gave me
this black and red scarf
which is the only thing of hers I have.
That is all I can tell you Mayra,
because after the guard caught her
I never heard anything again about Lorena.

CARTA-POEMA PARA NINFA VELEZ 'DIANA'

En el documental que vi esta noche en la televisión
descubrí tu rostro detrás de la pañoleta
que usabas en los operativos.
No pude equivocarme.
Eras vos misma.
Ese pelo que cuando corrías lo volaba el viento
era el mismo que yo había enredado en mis dedos
la noche de tu cumpleaños en Estelí
la misma noche que me contaste de tu participación
en las actividades clandestinas del Frente Sandinista de
        Liberación Nacional.
Recuerdo que esa noche te besé como nunca lo había
        hecho
y sentí por primera vez
más fuerte tu cuerpo entre mis brazos.
Ninfa no podría olvidarte
cómo hacerlo
si aún después de muerta siento que sos la misma
si aún así te quiero.
Siento egoístamente que vos engendraste esta
        Revolución;
quizá es por eso que la quiero tanto
como si descargando todo mi amor en ella
estuviera más cerca de vos.
Amar la Revolución es la manera más directa de
        serte fiel
es la mejor manera de amarte.
Estoy seguro que te sentirás feliz de ver los logros,
de participar en todas las tareas:

LETTER POEM FOR NINFA VÉLEZ 'DIANA'

In the documentary I watched last night on television
I discovered your face behind the scarf
you used to mask it with on missions.
I knew I was not mistaken.
It was you.
That hair that streamed in the wind as you ran
was the same I had wound between my fingers
the night of your birthday in Estelí
the same night you told me you were involved
in the clandestine activities of the Sandinista
      National Liberation Front.
I remember that night I kissed you as I never had
      before
and for the first time I felt
your body strong in my arms.
Ninfa I could not forget you
how could I
when even after you are dead I feel you are the same
and I still love you the same.
I feel selfishly that you gave birth to this
      Revolution;
perhaps that is why I love it so much
as if by putting all my love into it
I am nearer to you.
Loving the Revolution is the most direct way of being
      faithful to you
the best way of loving you.
I am sure you will feel happy to see our successes,
to share in all the tasks:

alfabetizando en las montañas del norte
a los campesinos
– 'ellos son nuestros,
nosotros debemos ser para ellos' –
me dijiste la noche de tu cumpleaños mientras
bailábamos.
Esa noche me di cuenta de una cosa:
más que amarte te admiraba
(ésa era mi manera revolucionaria de amarte).
Hablabas y fijabas tus ojos en el cielo
(los mismos que miraría brillar
una noche de lluvia en el parque de Condega
cuando se realizara nuestra definitiva despedida).
Es por eso que cuando veo un brigadista
luciendo su cotona gris y su mochila,
en mi mente, tu imagen de guerrillera es desplazada
por la imagen de alfabetizadora,
y te imagino contenta contándome tus
experiencias;
relacionando siempre tus tareas con nuestro amor,
como solías hacerlo.
Es inconcebible pensar que estés muerta.
Y es que para mí no lo estás.
Nadie muere en una revolución.
Morir en una revolución es revolucionar la vida,
es amar, sentir, vivir, dentro de una vida más profunda,
y vos Ninfa, has vuelto a nacer porque vivís allí
allí donde viven todos los revolucionarios
como Ernesto Castillo
Camilo Torres
José Benito Escobar.
Es por eso que así como te vi

teaching literacy in the northern mountains
    to the peasants
– 'they are ours,
we must be for them' –
you told me on your birthday night
    while we were dancing.
That night I realised something:
as well as loving you I admired you
(this was my revolutionary way of loving you).
You talked with your eyes looking up at the sky
              (those same eyes I saw shining
that rainy night in the Condega park
when we said goodbye for the last time).
That is why when I see a *brigadista*
resplendent in grey tunic and kitbag,
in my mind your image as a *guerrillera* gives way
to the image of you as a literacy teacher,
and I imagine you happily telling me about your
    experiences;
always connecting your work with our love,
as you used to do.
It is impossible to think you are dead.
Because for me you are not.
No one dies in a revolution.
Dying in a revolution means revolutionising life,
loving, feeling, living within a life that is more profound,
and you, Ninfa, have been reborn because you live there
where all the revolutionaries live
like Ernesto Castillo
        Camilo Torres
           José Benito Escobar.
So when I saw you like that

corriendo con el fusil levantado
                    (buscando una revolución)
trasluciendo tu belleza física
a través de la pantalla de televisión,
así siento que te veo muchas veces
y que me encuentro con vos
y que venís corriendo
con tu pelo suelto volando por el viento
y con los brazos abiertos para abrazarme
y que nos besamos,
como la noche de nuestra despedida.
Ninfa.
Amo la Revolución
ésa es la única manera de decirte que te quiero.

running with your gun raised

                        (trying to make a revolution)

your physical beauty shining

out through the television screen,

I feel I am often seeing you

and I am meeting you

and you come running

with your loose hair flying in the wind

and your arms open to hug me

and we kiss,

like the night we said goodbye.

Ninfa.

I love the Revolution

that's is my only way of telling you I love you.

CARLOS CALERO

LA LAGUNA DE MASAYA

Desde la Trompa del Cailagua el agua se divisa
y los chilamates enredados con el matapalo
como tocando el agua, embrocados
                              de lejos.
Pasan por el bajadero de Monimbó pescadores,
                              mujeres, chavalos.
En la orilla de la playa el plaas, plaas, plaas
de las lavanderas con los pezones morenos al aire.
(En el borde del gran hueco de la laguna
                              el viento zumba.)
Aguas que cambian de color según la época y el tiempo:
verde-plomo, plomo-verde,
claro-verde, verde-claro; verde, verde, verde.
También cambian las que lavan en las piedras:
llegan trigueñas, olorosas a sontol, ramalilas en el pelo
                              y a los meses
piel brillante, tostadas,
con el talayo cenizo y penetrado en sus manos
                              y en sus piernas.
Iguanas jelequemeñas, escamosas y panzonas
y garrobos bajo el sol agarrados de las peñas.
Abajo
el pescador en la poza o en el gamalote o en la costa
con su atarraya atisbando el cardumen de guabinas,
mojarras y guapotes-laguneros.
Zanates, tórtolas, pijules, chichiltotes
y güises se desprenden a beber desde
los guanacastes, jiñocuabos y pochotes.

CARLOS CALERO

LAKE MASAYA

You can see the lake from the top of the Waterfall
and where the laurel-leafed fig trees tangling
                              with the creepers
meet the water, from a distance they look upside down.
Through the Monimbó Gully fishermen pass,
                              women, children.
On the shoreline the *plass plass plass*
of the washerwomen with their brown nipples in the air.
(At the rim of the lake's great hollow the wind hums.)
Waters that change colour according to weather
                              and season:
lead-green, green-lead,
clear-green, green-clear; green, green, green.
The women washing on the stones also change:
they arrive light brown, smelling of cypress root,
                              with sprigs in their hair,
and after some months, their skin shines, toasted,
with the ashy washing water staining their hands
                              and legs.
Fat scaly iguanas and lizards
sunbathe clinging to boulders.
Down below, fishermen
in the water, among the tall grass, or along the shore,
stand with their nets in wait for the shoals of guabinas,
flounders and lake-herrings.
Grackles, turtle doves, wagtails, woodcock
and flycatchers come down to drink
from the conacaste, gumbo limbo and bombax trees.

Y en la tarde todo quieto.
Se van los pescadores, callados
pensando en la mujer, los chavalos. En la Revolución.
Las lavanderas suben por los bajaderos
lindas se ven en largos surcos
con motetes de ropa ajena en la cabeza

       jadeando

y se siente el olor a sontol
el olor a mujer.

And by evening everything is quiet.
The fishermen leave silently
thinking about their wives and children. The Revolution.
The washerwomen go up the gullies,
they look beautiful walking in long lines
with piles of other people's washing on their heads,
                                        panting
and you catch the smell of cypress root
the smell of woman.

GERARDO GADEA

EN LA ESCUELA MILITAR

Yo estaba de posta.
Los compañeros pasaban en largas filas marchando
                iban a clase.
Un zanate clarinero se posó en la rama de un malinche
a sombrear junto conmigo.
Gorjeaba
erizaba el plumaje negro
se sacudía
no dejaba de gorjear.
Parece que se aproxima el invierno.
En este mes de mayo
están florecidos los malinches
y el aire huele a esa flor.
Como los pájaros cuando llega el invierno
así nos alegramos en la Escuela Militar:
los compañeros tocan guitarra
cantan canciones revolucionarias
gritamos consignas a Sandino
                a Germán Pomares
                a Fonseca
                a la Revolución.
Los que hace tres meses vinieron a estudiar
                a la Carlos Agüero
– junto con los milicianos –
y ahora son oficiales-instructores
del Ejército Popular Sandinista
militarmente
                y en columnas

GERARDO GADEA

IN THE MILITARY SCHOOL

I was on guard.
The comrades were marching past in long lines
                    going to class.
A bugle-bird perched on a flame tree branch
to enjoy the shade with me.
It trilled
it bristled its black feathers
it shook itself
but did not stop trilling.
It seems winter is coming.
In this month of May
the flame trees are in flower
and the air smells of their blossom.
Like birds when winter comes
we too feel happy in the Military School:
the comrades play the guitar
sing revolutionary songs
we shout out chants to Sandino
                    Germán Pomares
                    Fonseca
                    the Revolution.
Those who came three months ago to study
                    at the Carlos Agüero
– together with the militia recruits –
and who are now officer-instructors
in the Sandinista People's Army
set out in military style
                    in columns

parten a sus regiones a defender la Revolución,
pero siguen viniendo estudiantes
con guitarras, consignas, canciones y poemas
a la Escuela Carlos Agüero
(como los pájaros cuando llega el invierno).

to their regions to defend the Revolution.
But students keep on coming
with guitars, chants, songs and poems
to the Carlos Agüero School
(like birds when winter comes).

CUANDO SEPAS

Cuando leás los poemas que he escrito para vos
te sentirás orgulloso.
Pero qué dirás cuando sepás
que los escribí para hacer referencia
de un pasado,
y que hoy
a quien doy mis besos y más
es a Rogelio
el sandinista.

CONY PACHECO

WHEN YOU KNOW

When you read the poems I have written for you
you will feel proud.
But what will you say when you know
I wrote them to refer
to the past,
and that today
the one I give my kisses to and more
is Rogelio
the Sandinista.

CIERTA DUDA DE AMOR

Te acostumbraste a mi forma de ser
de tal manera
que cuando te digo, amor,
que la Revolución necesita de nosotros
                    que me marche
vos me contestás:
                    – Estoy de acuerdo, camarada.
Y es entonces cuando siento
cierta duda de nuestro amor.

ISIDRO TERCERO

DOUBT

You have got used to my way of life
so that
when I tell you, love,
the Revolution requires of us
                    that I should go away
you answer me:
                    – Of course, comrade.
And that is when I feel
a certain doubt about our love.

ROSARIO MURILLO

MUJER EN LA REVOLUCION

¡Rara pasión la nuestra
circular con los ojos extrañados
maravillados de todo!
Cada veintiocho días, como un perro sin dueño
andar, las manos a la deriva
interrogando las más pequeñas cosas
la sombra de una campana o su mudez repentina
el vuelo abierto de los pájaros
la inevitable tristeza de una anciana,
lila, como la muerte.
Extraño rito, cada veintiocho días incendiarte
                    la sangre
como un ciclo de amor en el amor
como un ciclo de luz en la poesía
como una ventana abierta al paso de los funerales
al aire de los nacimientos.
Vivo una renovación de la sangre
– cada veintiocho días –
porque soy mujer y amo y me doy cuenta
y cada veintiocho días nazco nueva
cuando renuevo la sangre
cuando hay nuevos mundos febriles azotando
cuando nace un óvulo, un huevo, un átomo,
                    un principio de vida
me alumbro, me doy a luz
pero mi propia vida
entre mil otras cosas importantes
como amar, dar un beso, ver reír a los niños.

ROSARIO MURILLO

WOMAN IN THE REVOLUTION

What a strange passion ours is,
going round with staring eyes
wondering at everything!
Every twenty-eight days, like a stray dog,
wandering about, with floppy hands,
questioning the smallest things,
a bell's shadow or sudden dumbness,
the birds' trajectory,
an old woman's inevitable sadness,
lilac as death.
Strange rite, every twenty-eight days for your blood
                    to kindle
like a cycle of love within love
a cycle of light within poetry,
like a window open to passing funerals,
to the air of births.
I have a renewal of blood
– every twenty-eight days –
because I am a woman and I love and am aware
and every twenty-eight days I am born afresh
when I renew my blood
when there are new worlds feverishly whipping
when an ovule, an egg, an atom,
                    a principle of life is born.
I set myself alight, I give birth to myself,
but my own life
among a thousand other important things
like loving, kissing, seeing children laugh

y aceptar hacer a un lado la poesía
– la luz
el universo –
para ponerme seria
y seguir, apurada
construyendo la luz, el universo.

and accepting that poetry
– light
universe –
must be done on the side,
in order to become serious and hurry on
creating light, the universe.

ACONTECIO EN UN VIAJE DE DOMINGO EN LA PLAYA

Llovía.
Nosotros pensábamos optimistas:
El camino se aclarará más adelante.
Seguramente en la playa, el sol.

El parabrisas del carro zas zas.
Neblina en las ventanas.
Árboles envueltos en sábanas blancas.
Gente mojada.
Frío en la carretera.

– Mejor estaríamos en la cama.
   El horizonte hacia el lado del mar está todo nebuloso.
   Devolvámonos a leer y abrazarnos.

Giramos.
Entramos a Diriamba.
Todo el pueblo encerrado
guardado de la bruma la llovizna.

En el enredo de las esquinas
desembocamos de improviso en una rotonda:
Un monumento nombres de compañeros.
El cementerio al fondo.
Se veía hermoso.
Niebla suavizando la muerte.

GIOCONDA BELLI

IT HAPPENED ONE SUNDAY
ON A TRIP TO THE BEACH

It was raining.
We took an optimistic view:
It will clear up later.
It is sure to be sunny at the beach.

Swish! Swish! against the car's windscreen.
Fog on the windows.
Trees wrapped in white sheets.
People getting wet.
Cold on the road.

– We should have stayed in bed.
   The horizon towards the sea is all foggy.
   Let's go back and read and cuddle up.

We turned round.
We entered Diriamba.
Everyone indoors
sheltering from the drizzling cloud.

Driving through the tangle of streets
we suddenly came upon a roundabout.
A monument with comrades' names.
The cemetery in the background.
It looked beautiful.
Mist softening death.

– Bajemos. Nunca he estado aquí.
Quisiera ver la tumba de Ricardo Morales.
Dejarle algunas caricias sobre la tierra.
Unas hojitas de limonaria.

Bajamos.
Las tumbas de los ricos imponentes a la entrada.
Sus ángeles llorando lágrimas de lluvia.
Llovizna y tumbas buscando a Ricardo.
¿Dónde estará Ricardo?
Y encontramos lápidas de otros:
combatientes, padres, hermanos, monjas octogenarias.
Hasta una mezquita oriental con este epitafio:
'Aquí yace Ramón López
que murió joven
disfrazado de anciano.'
Pensamos en la muerte.
Yo, Ricardo buscaba tus ojos.
Aquellos que unas pocas veces vi, inolvidables.
Los ojos de tu hija, Doris María.

No te encontramos.
Regresamos bajo la llovizna pertinaz.
Fue como tocar la puerta de tu casa
y no hallarte.
Como que alguien dijera que habías salido,
que andabas en alguna reunión.

Fue como saber que tu tumba no existe,
que andás por allí,
apurado entre las calles mojadas
trabajando sin morirte nunca.

– Let's get out. I have never been here.
I should like to see Ricardo Morales' tomb.
Leave him some remembrance on his grave.
A few sprigs of lemon.

We got out.
The imposing tombs of the rich at the entrance.
Their angels weeping tears of rain.
Searching for Ricardo among the dripping tombstones.
Where can Ricardo be?
And we found other stones:
combatants, parents, brothers, eighty-year-old nuns.
Even a miniature mosque with this epitaph:
'Here lies Ramón López,
who died young
disguised as an old man.'
We thought about death.
Ricardo, I looked for your eyes.
Those unforgettable eyes I saw only a few times.
The eyes of your daughter, Doris María.

We did not find you.
We went home through the persistent rain.
It was like knocking at the door of your house
and not finding you in.
As if someone were to say you had gone out,
gone to some meeting.

It was like discovering your tomb does not exist,
and you still hurry about there,
walking the wet streets,
working and not dying ever.

SEGUIREMOS NACIENDO

Estás allá,
de pie en la plaza.
Estamos las dos,
mujeres,
una frente a la otra
bajo la intensa mirada de Carlos,
bajo el cielo dorado de la tarde
y toco la eternidad con mis dos manos.

Me toco y te toco
cuando firmemente pronunciás tu juramento,
cuando jurás ser valiente
> ser como Brenda Rocha combatiendo
> y sonriendo
> ser digna militante de la juventud
> sandinista.

No sé donde termina mi sangre y empieza la tuya.
La plaza es como un gigantesco vientre dando a luz
y mi carne se nace de nuevo para parirte,
ahora que has germinado
– muchacha amapola
arrancada del Universo
brotada del fondo de mi cuerpo.

Dada a luz estás
hoy que tus ojos brillan
y aman los grandes nombres
la dulce sencillez de nuestro pueblo.

WE SHALL GO ON BEING BORN

There you are,
standing in the square.
We both are,
two women
facing one another
under Carlos' searching gaze,
under the golden evening sky
and I touch eternity with my two hands.

I touch myself and you
when you firmly make your oath,
swearing to be brave
                    to be like Brenda Rocha fighting
                              and smiling,
                    to be a militant worthy
                              of the Sandinista youth.

I don't know where my blood ends and yours begins.
The square is like a huge womb giving birth
and my flesh is reborn to deliver you
now you have germinated
– poppy girl
seed from the universe
who sprouted in me.

You are born into light
as today your eyes shine
loving our great names
and our people's simple kindness.

Llena de luz te veo
y la piel se me enciende de orgullo
y el pecho se me invade de campanas
anunciando este parto jubiloso.

Ven y dame la mano,
esa tu mano joven, militante.
Ahora que nos unen Revolución y sangre
enfrentaremos juntas
este futuro de guerra y de victoria
y cuando amés a un hombre
y también brote la vida de tu vida,
naceremos otra vez,
muchas veces,
prolongando roja nuestra bandera;
hija,
mujer,
compañera
Maryam.

I see you full of light
and my skin glows with pride
and my breasts are pealing bells
announcing this happy birth.

Come and give me your hand,
your young militant's hand.
Now we are joined by blood and Revolution
together we shall face
future war and victory
and when you love a man
and life springs from your life too,
we shall be born again,
many times,
keeping our flag red
daughter,
woman,
comrade
Maryam.

NICARAGUA AGUA FUEGO

Lluvia
Ventana trae agua sobre hojas
viento pasa arrastrando faldas
lodos llevan troncos
árboles pintan estrellas charcos de sangre
fronteras de un día que hay que pelear
sin remedio sin más alternativa que la lucha
Detrás de cortina mojada
escribo dedos sobre gatillos
guerras grandes
dolores tamaño ojos de madres
goteando aguaceros incontenibles
vienen los cuerpecitos helados muertos
bajan de la montaña los muchachos
con sus hamacas recuperadas de la contra
comemos poco hay poco queremos comer todos
manos grandes blancas quieren matarnos
pero hicimos hospitales camas
donde mujeres gritan nacimientos
todo el día pasamos palpitando
tum tum tam tam
venas de indios repiten historia:
No queremos hijos que sean esclavos
flores salen de ataúdes
nadie muere en Nicaragua
Nicaragua mi amor mi muchachita violada
levantándose componiéndose la falda
caminando detrás del asesino siguiéndolo
montaña abajo montaña arriba
no pasarán dicen los pajaritos

NICARAGUA WATER FIRE

Rain
Window drips on leaves
wind whips skirts
mud loosens tree-trunks
trees sketch star pools of blood
edges of a day that must be fought
no help for it no alternative but the struggle
Behind the damp curtain
I finger triggers
great wars
pain the size of mothers' eyes
unstoppable torrents
the small frozen dead bodies come
the lads come down from the mountains
with their hammocks recovered from the contra
we eat little there is little we all want to eat
big white hands want to kill us
but we made hospital beds
where women cry out births
we spend all day with pounding hearts
tum tum tam tam
Indian pulses repeat history:
We don't want children who'll be slaves
flowers bloom out of coffins
no one dies in Nicaragua
Nicaragua my love my raped girl
standing up and tidying her skirt
going after the murderer following him
uphill and downhill
they shall not pass say the small birds

no pasarán dicen los amantes que hacen el amor
que hacen hijos que hacen pan que hacen trincheras
que hacen uniformes que hacen cartas
        para los movilizados
Nicaragua mi amor mi negra miskita suma rama
palo de mayo en la Laguan de Perlas
vientos huracanados bajando San Juan abajo
no pasarán y llueve sobre los sombreritos
que andan husmeando el rastro de las bestias
y no les dan descanso los persiguen los sacan
del pecho de la patria los arrancan sacan la hierba mala
no la dejan que pegue
queremos maíz arroz frijoles
que peguen las semillas en las tierras donde
campesino guarda en caja de madera titulo
        de Reforma Agraria
no pasen los diablos anunciando la buena nueva
        del perdón
a los que vieron ranchos arder
y vecino asesinado frente a su mujer y sus hijos
Nicaragua mi muchachita
baila sabe leer platica con la gente
le cuenta su cuento sale en aviones a contar su cuento
anda por todo el mundo con su cuento a tuto
habla hasta por los codos en periódicos de idiomas
        incomprensibles
grita se pone brava furiosa
parece mentira cuánta bulla mete
        y cómo resiste
aviones minas pirañas bombas maldiciones en inglés
discursos sobre cómo bajar la cabeza
y no se deja se suelta pega carreras

they shall not pass say the lovers making love
making children making bread making trenches
making uniforms making letters
    to soldiers
Nicaragua my love my black Miskito Sumu Rama
maypole in the Lake of Pearls
hurricane hurtling down San Juan
they shall not pass as it rains on the caps
of those who sniff out the trail of the brutes
and give them no rest follow them pull them
off the country's breast tear them out get rid of the weeds
don't let them take root
we want maize rice beans
for the seeds to set in the earth
where the peasant keeps in a wooden box
    his Land Reform title deed
don't let the devils pass announcing good news
    of forgiveness
to those who saw farms burn
and neighbour murdered in front of his wife and children
Nicaragua my little girl
she dances she can read talk to people
tell them her story travels in aeroplanes to tell her story
all over the world with her story
speaks till words come out of her elbows in newspapers
    in incomprehensible languages
shouts gets angry gets furious
sounds boastful with the racket she makes
    and how she resists
planes mines piranhas bombs curses in English
speeches on how to bow her head
and she will not she breaks free and races on

y allá va el General y la colina los cohetes reactivos
las columnas verdes avanzando despalando
haciendo ingenios de azúcar
ríos de leche casas escuelas
chavalos contando su historia
renqueando salidos del hospital
agarrando bus para volver al norte
viento que se sacude el miedo
nacimos para esto
reímos para esto
entre dientes andamos la rabia y la esperanza
no nos dejan no los dejamos ni a sol ni a sombra
país chiquito pero cumplidor
Nicaragua lanza lanzada atrevida chúcara yegua
potreros de Chontales donde Nadine
sueña caballos percherones
y soñamos en surtidor
tenemos una fábrica de sueños
sueños en serie para los descreidos
aquí nadie sale sin su arañazo en la conciencia
nadie pasa sin que le pase nada
país de locos iluminados poetas pintores
chorros de luces escuelas de danza
conferencias internacionales salones de protocolo
policías escolares regañando dulcemente
carne y hueso de gente que acierta y se equivoca
que prueba y vuelve a probar
aquí todo se mueve caderas de mujer bailando
sonando ganas de vivir ante momias
hablando de la muerte queriendo ganar su pasaje
     de regreso
en hojas impresas que salen por la tarde con sus mentiras

and there goes the General and the hill the rockets
green columns advancing clearing the ground
making sugar mills
rivers of milk houses schools
children telling their history
limping out of hospital
catching the bus back up north
wind that shakes off fear
we are born for this
we laugh for this
fury and hope between clenched teeth
they won't let us be so we won't let them in sun or shade
a tiny country but yes we do it
Nicaragua hurls is hurled she is bold a wild pony
Chontales pastures where Nadine dreams
of Percherón horses
and we are dream-makers
we have a dream factory
whole series of dreams for unbelievers
here no one goes out with awareness unscathed
no one goes by without being involved
country of mad lit poets and painters
light streams dance schools
international conferences protocol rooms
student police scolding gently
flesh and bone people who make certain make mistakes
try and try again
here everything moves like a woman's hips dancing
while life lasts let's feel alive
speaking of death wanting their return ticket
in printed broadsheets that come out in the afternoon
      with their lies

y sus rabias de histérica frustrada
envidia de la muchacha que se contonea, se chiquea
cierra el ojo vende tamales vende pinturas
hace milicias va al parque inventa el amor
enciende los malinches se esconde para desconcertar
sale andando en medio de bayonetas caladas
hace circo y ferias y reza
y cree en la vida y en la muerte
y alista espadas de fuego
para que a nadie le quede más decisión
que paraíso terrenal
o cenizas
patria libre
o morir.

and their furies of frustrated hysteria
envying the girl who sways her body provokes
winks sells *tamales* sells paintings
does her bit in the militia goes to the park invents love
sets the flame trees alight flirts playing hide and seek
walks out among fixed bayonets
makes circus makes holiday prays
and believes in living and dying
brandishes her fiery sword
to ensure the only choice for anyone
is heaven on earth
or ashes
a free country
or death.

CARLOS MARTÍNEZ RIVAS

BIENVENIDO, MONSEÑOR

Para Monseñor Obando

Bienvenido.

Sólo que van a faltar algunos en la recepción.

No estarán las madres nicaragüenses
por cuyos hijos muertos en combate
no se dignó decir una abierta oración
Su Santidad Juan Pablo II
                         (se hizo un silencio
en la Plaza por espacio de un segundo ensanchado,
                                 eterno.
Aún sigue suspendido ese silencio, estoy oyéndolo.
Pero no cedió el Pontifice. Se mantuvo firme).

No van a estar esos muchachos hijos de esas madres,
ni otras madres de otros hijos muertos después:
caídos durante tu reciente visita al Vaticano
con el propósito de consolidar en Roma,
Capital de la Cristiandad, tus relaciones
con Washington, la Capital del Capital.
No estarán presentes en tu Bienvenida.

Echarás de menos a los niños
de la Alianza de Niños Sandinistas.
No estará Luis Alfonso Velázquez Flores con flores

CARLOS MARTÍNEZ RIVAS

WELCOME, MONSENOR

For Monseñor Obando

Welcome.

But some will be missing from the reception.

The Nicaraguan mothers won't be there
for whose children killed in combat
His Holiness John Paul II
did not deign to pray in public
(there was a silence
in the Square for the space of a lengthy, unending
second.
That silence is still going on, I can hear it.
But the Pope did not give in. He stood firm).

Neither will those boys, those mothers' sons be there
nor other mothers of other children who died after them:
killed during your recent visit to the Vatican
with the intention of consolidating in Rome,
the Capital of Christianity, your relations
with Washington, the Capital of Capital.
They will not be present at your welcome.

You will be without the children
from the Sandinista Children's Alliance.
Luis Alfonso Velásquez Flores won't be there
with flowers

para ti. Ni el muerto ni los vivos ni los que van
a morir (*morituri*) te saludarán.
Te van hacer falta los mimados del Evangelio.

Te recibirán solamente los Magnates.
The last tycoons! Los últimos magnates.
La Alta Curia. El Alto Clero. La Altísima
                                                    Bajeza.

Y claro, tu feligresía adormilada.
Los que según Jesús integran el rebaño ciego:
'Vine al mundo para que los que no veían vean,
y los que creen ver se vuelvan ciegos' (*Juan* 9:39).

Escribimos de nuevo lo que vimos y vivimos
hartos veinte años pero tan actual
como el diario inédito de mañana: 'Antes
de que hayas empañado la Mitra, alzándola
entre tus temblorosos dedos pastorales
en defensa de la opresión...',
                                    recapacita,
Pastor. Te recibirán los ciegos,
tu grey hija del sueño. La Armada del Miedo.

No mirarán tu pompa los despiertos. Ellos
lejos pecho a tierra,
corazón batiendo
avizoran al agresor en la frontera.

Perdona su ausencia en tu Bienvenida. Absuélvelos.

for you. Neither the dead nor the living nor those
who are about to die (*morituri*) will salute you.
The Gospel's favourites will be missing.

Only the Magnates will receive you.
The last tycoons! The ultimate big businessmen!
The High Curia. The High Clergy. The Most High
                                        Baseness.

And of course, your drowsy faithful.
Those who according to Jesus make up the blind flock:
'I came into the world so that those who couldn't see
                                        might see
and those who think they can see become blind'
                                        (*John* 9:39).
Again we write what we have seen and endured
for twenty long years, but still news
like tomorrow's unpublished paper: 'Before
you soil the Mitre, by raising it
in your trembling pastoral fingers
in defence of oppression...', reflect,
Pastor. You will be welcomed by the blind
Your dream-led flock. The Army of Fear.

Those who are awake will not watch your pomp. They
are far away, crawling along the ground
with beating hearts
on guard for the aggressor at the frontier.

Forgive their absence from your welcome.
                        Absolve them.

JULIO VALLE-CASTILLO

LA PASION
SEGUN LAS VECINAS

**A las madres de todos los secuestrados
y en memoria de José Mendoza**

Y la pobre señora con sus orejas frías, a pesar de que el
hijo siempre le dio problemas: pequeño se le perdió, hace
como cuatro años, la huelga de hambre: 40 días y 40
noches, y estos últimos tiempos en esa organisación, en
esa banda, en malas compañias: con hombres y mujeres de
lo peor.

Unos de esos hombres fue el que vino avisarle a Doña
María.
No. No fue Pedro, el viejo calvo, vende-pescado.
A ese no se la ha vuelto a ver ni la cara.
Fue un jovencito, barba-cerrada, bien afeitado...

Y esa familia no tiene nada, mucha menos dinero para
pagar un abogado.
Si el señor, el marido, el papá del muchacho era
carpintero.

Yo me acuerdo del muchachito con su cotón largo
jugando sobre banco de la carpintería, entre las tablas,
entre las trozas aserradas, con el colochero de la madera.

Esa casa era una fragancia: olía a sándalo y sabía a cedro
verde, amargo...

JULIO VALLE-CASTILLO

THE PASSION
ACCORDING TO THE NEIGHBOURS

**To the mothers of all the kidnapped
and in memory of José Mendoza**

And the poor woman whose ears are not burning, although
her son always caused her problems: when he was small
they lost him, and about four years ago, he went on hunger
strike: 40 days and 40 nights, and lately he's been in that
organisation, that gang, bad company: with men and
women of the worst sort.

One of those men was the one who came to tell Doña
María.
No. It wasn't Peter, the bald old fishmonger.
We never saw his face again.
It was a young man, with a thick beard, well-trimmed...

And that family's got nothing, never mind money to pay a
lawyer.
Seeing as her husband, the boy's father, was a carpenter.

I remember the little lad with his long shirt playing on the
carpentry bench, among the planks, the sawn wood and
the shavings.

That house was fragrant: it smelt of sandalwood and tasted
of green cedar, bitter...

Puro aserrín rojo.

El hijo de la señora debe de andar por los 32 o 33 años
porque el mayor de mis hijos y él son contemporáneos.

A mi nunca me simpatizó ese muchacho: con las mechas
largas y barbado y hablando mal de las personas
honorables. Diciendo sólo locuras. La otra vez en el
templo hizo un escándalo.

Dicen que andaba metido en una cuestión de armas...

Y uno de ellos mismos fue quien lo delató a la Guardia. Es
lo que siempre pasa.

El hijo de la señora estuvo preso y deben de haberlo
torturado, lo trajeron y llevaron de la Casa de Caifás a los
Tribunales y hasta a la propia Embajada, me dijo un
taxista.

La verdad es que ese muchacho mucho hablaba,
andaba calentándole la cabeza a la gente,
con unas sus ideas exóticas, extrañas.

Yo nunca dejé que mi hijo se le acercara.
Mi marido vino un día asustado contándome
que lo escuchó decir en un discurso cerca del pueblo,
ya casi a la entrada, que quien perdía todo,
todo lo encontraba en la casa de su padre.

Si esa gente no tiene nada.
Un periodista me contó que la señora pasó al pie de la

Pure red sawdust.

Her son must be about 32 or 33 because my oldest son and
he are the same age.

I never took to that boy: with his long curls and beard and
speaking badly of decent people. A load of rubbish he
talked. That other time in the temple he caused a scandal.

They say he is mixed up in something to do with arms...

And it was one of them who gave him away to the Guard.
That's always the way.

The woman's son was arrested and they must have
tortured him, they took him and brought him to Caiphas'
house, before the Courts and even to the Embassy, a taxi
driver told me.

The truth is that boy talked too much,
he went about putting things into people's heads,
some of his weird ideas.

I never let my son go near him.
My husband came one day quite shocked and told me
that he had heard him make a speech near the village,
just where it begins, saying those who lost everything
would find it all again in his father's house.

But those people have got nothing.
A journalist told me the woman stood at the foot of the

cruz todo el tiempo sólo acompañada por el jovencito
barba-cerrada y una mujer pelo largo...

Quién sabe entonces como irán hacer ahora.
Ojalá y el Coronel no les ponga muchas trabas para
entregarles el cadáver.

¿Y tendrán tumba en el cementerio, sudario?
Pobre la señora y tan hermoso que era su muchacho.

Managua, abril de 1989

cross the whole time with only the young bearded man
and some woman with long hair to keep her company...

So who knows how they will manage now?
Let's hope the Colonel doesn't make too much trouble
about handing over the body to them.

And will they have a grave in the cemetery, a shroud?
Poor woman and her boy was so good looking.

Managua, April 1989

BALADA DEL DESERTOR

Hoy amaneció la novedad en el vecindario:
Trajeron a un muchacho del Servicio Militar Patriótico
en su liso ataúd de soldado.

                      Este domingo anduvo
franco de la base militar
y bajó a un mineral fantasma de Chontales
y escuchó unos cuentos terroríficos de la Contra
                 y se echó a correr seguido de miedo
hasta la locura, hasta el pavor
              hasta el escalofrío de sentirse
                 horas después de capturado
a la cabeza del batallón con la cabeza rapada
              hacia el frente de guerra
              hacia la primera línea de fuego
cuando le voló la pierna una mina norteamericana.

El sanitario dio los primeros auxilios.
Pero sus compañeros no pudieron llegar a tiempo
                 al hospital de campaña.

Dicen que no es héroe. Es desertor.
Dicen que no es mártir, el desangrado.

El pánico tiene aún al muchacho frío.
Cada vez se pone más helado y más pálido,
su lividez lo funde con la sábana.

Se quedó como un cirio
que se vela en un rincón a sí mismo,
al saberse despernancado y desbanderado, solo, íngrimo

BALLAD OF THE DESERTER

This morning the neighbourhood saw something new:
They brought home a boy on military service
in his plain soldier's coffin.
                              Last Sunday
he went missing from the camp
descended in search of dream-waters in Chontales
and heard horrifying tales about the Contra.
                    He began to run driven by fear,
crazed with terror, panic-stricken,
                    till shuddering he found himself
                              captured some hours later
with shaven head, at the head of the battalion
                    on its way to the war front,
                    on its way to the line of fire.
Then a North American mine blew off his leg.

The medic gave first aid.
But his comrades could not get him to the field hospital
                              in time.

They say he is not a hero. He is a deserter.
They say he is not a martyr, though he bled to death.

Panic still grips the cold boy.
He grows colder and paler,
his livid colour matches the sheet.

White as a wax candle
in the corner, keeping vigil for himself,
knowing he is crippled, deserted, alone, on his own

a lo largo de todo su segundo día de muerto
porque la hermana y la madre
llegarán al país hasta en el vuelo de las 6
$\qquad$ de la tarde.

Dicen que no es héroe ni mártir.
Lo sepultarán sin honores militares.
Es desertor y los dersertores...
Pero qué hago yo,
qué hacemos con su sangre.

Managua, junio de 1989

all through the second day of his death
because his sister and mother
will not arrive in the country till the 6 o'clock
afternoon flight.

They say he is not a hero or martyr.
They will bury him without military honours.
He is a deserter and deserters....
But what shall I do,
what shall we do with his blood?

Managua, June 1989

TARJETA POSTAL
AL CAPITAN BOSCO CENTENO

**San Carlos
Río San Juan
Nicaragua. A.C.**

En este hotel de montaña en Donovaly
escuché otra versión de aquel tu poema
sobre el guerrillero caído en Nueva Guinea:

Desenterrado después del triúnfo
encontraron todo un cadáver florecido:
los granos de maíz germinaban mazorcas
doradas por los bolsillos del uniforme.

Pasó igual con la caballera de Arlen Siú:
mientras estuvo sepultada fue raigambre
del árbol que anida las lunas en El Sauce.

Resulta que Miklós Radnóti (1909-1944),
niño huérfano y húngaro,
muerto en campo de concentración,
sólo fue identificado en la fosa común,
porque en su chaqueta de presidiario
que mal lo libró del frío,
                    y acaso del escalofrío final
hallaron las *Églogas* y *Tarjetas Postales*, un manojo
de cuartillas: hojas verdes, frescas de poesía.

Donovaly, 25 de septiembre de 1984

POSTCARD
TO CAPTAIN BOSCO CENTENO

San Carlos
Río San Juan
Nicaragua, Central America

In this mountain hotel in Donovaly
I heard another version of that poem you wrote
about the guerrilla who fell in Nueva Guinea:

When they dug him up after the Triumph
they found his whole corpse had sprouted,
and through his uniform pockets
the maize grains had germinated golden cobs.

The same thing happened with Arlen Siú's long hair:
when she was buried, it became rootstock
of the nesting-tree for the El Sauce moon.

It appears that Miklós Radnóti (1909-1944),
a Hungarian orphan,
who died in a concentration camp,
was only identified in the common grave,
because in his convict jacket,
which barely protected him from the cold,
       much less the final shudder,
they found *Eclogues* and *Postcards*,
a handful of papers: fresh green leaves of poetry.

Donovaly, Hungary, 25 September 1984

VIDALUZ MENESES

TRABAJO VOLUNTARIO

Dejamos los escritorios,
los memorandums y los informes
para marchar a los cafetales.

Las mujeres recordamos los meses de embarazo
cuando nos amarramos las canastas a la cintura
y aumentamos paulatinamente su peso
en la recogida del café.

Disfrutamos la naturaleza
cortando de arbustos agobiados
bolitas rojas y brillantes parecidas a cerezas;
otras oscurecidas con la maduración
adquieren el tono de las uvas
y hasta su roce con las yemas de los dedos
tienta la imaginación.
Los sazones amarillos o verdosos, ovalados o redondos
como peras y tomates diminutos.
En los surcos de repela
quedan dispersos los granos.
Unos negros y arrugados como pasas
y otros duros calcinados como semillas.

En ese paraíso frutal,
se desliza verde sobre la rama verde
el temible chichicaste.
Cuando te ataca, su dolor es como de
                    inyección de aceite.

VIDALUZ MENESES

VOLUNTARY WORK

We leave our desks,
the memos and reports
to go to the coffee fields.

We women recall the months of pregnancy
as we tie the baskets to our waists
and gradually increase their weight
by filling them with coffee.

We enjoy nature,
cutting the cherry-like shining red
berries from laden bushes;
some have ripened
to the colour of black grapes
and just brushing them with fingertips
tempts the imagination.
The ripening yellow or green ones, oval or round
are like tiny pears and tomatoes.
Grains lie scattered
on the ground for gleaning.
Some are black and wrinkled as raisins
others are like hard seeds.

In this fruity paradise,
green along the green branch
slithers the fearful nettle.
When it attacks you the pain stings
                like injected oil.

La sabiduría del campo descubrió que en él
están la vida y la muerte,
que su excremento verde, intenso
se vierte sobre el piquete
para quitar el dolor y evitar la fiebre.

Recoger café como algodón
es regresar a nuestras raíces
cuando nuestro primeros padres cosecharon el cacao.

El café y el algodón son ahora nuestra moneda.

1983

Country wisdom discovered
it had both life and death in it,
that its deep green juice
can be rubbed on the sting
to cure the pain and avoid fever.

Gathering coffee, and cotton,
means returning to our roots
when our first parents harvested cocoa.

Coffee and cotton are our currency now.

1983

MURO DE LAMENTACIONES

Esta vez no ahogaré la memoria,
asumiré los muertos y la separación de los amantes
que es otra forma de morir.
No deambularé esquizofrénica por el mundo
sino con el estandarte del holocausto vivido,
no ahogaré sus voces que claman por el reino que
no hemos podido construir,
no ignoraré la sangre en el barro,
el alarido del fondo de las entrañas,
el rugido de la multitud acumulado en el pecho,
la furia de los impotentes,
el mal gusto de gritar en una calle contra las
impecables paredes,
la punzada directa en el corazón
al detenernos en un semáforo.
No pondré diques al llanto
ni pesaré las palabras en el fiel de la balanza
– la mediocrita áurea hecha trizas,
la mesura apartada por inútil –
sin tributos ni mayores concesiones a la vida.
Hay un tiempo de llorar que debe ser cumplido
hasta el hundimiento total. Valle de lágrimas,
Muro de lamentaciones,
rasgadura de velos para que salga el ánima
y se exponga en la piedra de sacrificio,
hora en que el náufrago suelte su asidero de vida,
hora del despliegue de la orfandad ante el final
más allá de los visto y vivido, más allá.

1990

WAILING WALL

This time I will not stifle the memory,
I will take on the dead and the separation of lovers
which is another kind of dying.
I will not wander schizophrenetically through the world
but stand by the holocaust we have suffered.
I will not stifle their voices crying for the kingdom
we have not been able to build,
I will not ignore the blood on the ground
the shriek from the guts,
the pent-up roar of the crowd,
the fury of the powerless,
the distaste at shouting in a street
against impeccable walls,
the direct blow to the heart
as we stop at a traffic light.
I will set no limits to our mourning
neither will I weigh words in the balance
– golden mediocrity torn to shreds,
the scales discarded as useless –
I will make no concessions.
There is a time for weeping which must be got through
until the sinking is complete. Valley of tears,
Wall of lamentations,
tearing of veils for the soul to appear
and offer itself on the stone of sacrifice,
the hour at which the shipwreck releases its grasp on life,
the ultimate hour of orphaning,
beyond anything we have seen and endured, beyond it.

1990

EPILOGUE

CANTO DE LOS NICARAGUAS

Cuando se mete el sol mi señor, mi señor,
me duele, me duele el corazón.
Murió, no vive el sol,
el fuego del día.
Te quiero, yo te quiero
fuego del día, sol no te vayas.
Mi corazón, mi corazón llora.
Fuego del día no te vayas,
no te vayas fuego.
Se fue el sol.
Mi corazón llora.

Anon, Nahuatl, 16th Century
Spanish version by Angel María Garibay

SONG OF THE NICARAGUAS

When the sun sets, my lord, my lord,
my heart hurts, it hurts.
The sun, the fire of day
has died, it is not alive.
I love you, I love you
day-fire, sun do not go.
My heart, my heart cries.
Day-fire do not go away,
fire do not go.
The sun has gone.
My heart cries.

Anon, Nahuatl, 16th Century

ERNESTO CARDENAL

EN LA TUMBA DEL GUERRILLERO

Pienso en tu cuerpo que se ha ido desbaratando
                              bajo la tierra
haciéndose suave tierra, humus otra vez
junto con el humus de todos los demás humanos
que han existido y existirán en la bolita del mundo
haciéndonos todos juntos tierra fértil del planeta Tierra.
Y cuando los cosmonautas miren esta bola azul y rosa
                            en la noche negra
lo que estarán mirando, lejos, es tu luminosa tumba
                (tu tumba y la de todos)
y cuando los extraterrestres desde alguna parte
                miren este punto de luz de la Tierra
estarán mirando tu tumba.
Y un día será todo tumba, silenciosa tumba,
y ya no habrá más seres vivos en el planeta
                            compañero.
                ¿Y después?
Después nos desbarataremos más, volaremos,
                        átomos en el cosmos.
Y tal vez la materia es eterna hermano
sin principio ni fin o tiene un fin
                y recomienza cada vez.
Tu amor sí tuvo un comienzo pero no tiene final.
Y tus átomos que estuvieron en el suelo de Nicaragua,
tus átomos amorosos, que dieron la vida por amor,
ya verás, serán luz,
me imagino tus partículas en la vastedad del cosmos
como pancartas, como afiches vivos.

ERNESTO CARDENAL

THE GUERRILLA'S TOMB

I think of your body that has been rotting
                              underground
becoming good earth, humus again
together with the humus of all the other humans
who have existed and will exist in the ball of the earth
all becoming fertile earth of the planet Earth.
And when the cosmonauts look at this blue and pink ball
in the black night
what they will be seeing, far off, is your luminous tomb
            (your tomb and everybody's)
and when extraterrestrials from somewhere
            see this point of light that is Earth
they will be looking at your tomb.
And one day it will be all tomb, a silent tomb
and there will no longer be living beings on the planet
                              comrade.
            And then?
When we have disintegrated further, we shall fly,
                  as atoms in the cosmos.
And perhaps matter is eternal brother
without beginning or end or it ends
            and keeps beginning again.
Yes, your love did have a beginning but it has no end.
And your atoms which were in the soil of Nicaragua,
your loving atoms, that gave their life for love,
you'll see, they will be light.
I imagine your particles in the vastness of the cosmos
like placards, like living posters.

No sé si me explico.
Lo que sé es que nunca se olvidará tu nombre
y para siempre se gritará: ¡Presente!

I don't know if I am explaining myself.
What I do know is that your name
will never be forgotten
and for evermore you will be acclaimed: *Presente!*

POSTSCRIPT

From: *Confession of Love*

When they killed Eduardo Contreras, when they killed Camilo Ortega, Israel Lewites, so many other comrades, I never cried. I swallowed my tears of despair and frustration. Neither did I cry when my father died, or my elder sister Luisa, even though the sorrow of it washed over me like a blind tide that found no outlet in tears, and my jaws were set. The long repressed cry of my whole life broke out that early morning, which came on top of all those hours of sorrow and made it the saddest of my whole life.

At six in the morning I was to join Daniel in the Olaf Palme Conference Centre to accompany him in his public appearance. On leaving the house, I met Ernesto Cardenal, my neighbour in the street, who was always up and about early and had gone to bed confident of victory.

'Is it certain that we have lost the elections?' he asked me in astonishment.

I told him it was, that everything was lost, there was nothing to be done. And I left him sitting in the gutter, with his face in his hands, sunk in his own solitude and his own thoughts...

*

There was to be no more crying. Real revolutions do not die. The month of May was coming. Soon the rains would arrive to deck the desolate country and restore their greenness to trees and leaves.

And under the earth, in their furrows, the seeds of our dead lie waiting to germinate again. They will speak to us once more with their voices of hope and the joy of new fruits.

OUTLINE CHRONOLOGY 1954-1990

Names of poets whose work is translated in this book are given in bold.

1954

Apr   APRIL CONSPIRACY. A group of conspirators, including **Ernesto Cardenal**, Pedro Joaquín Chamorro and Arturo Cruz attempt to overthrow the dictator Somoza García and take over the presidential palace. The action fails. Those captured are tortured; Pablo de Leal has his tongue cut out. Adolfo Báez Bone is castrated and then killed. The veteran of Sandino's army, the shoemaker Optaciano Morazán, is also killed.

1956

Sep 21 ASSASSINATION OF SOMOZA I. The poet **Rigoberto López Pérez** assassinates the dictator Anastasio Somoza García. For the week that the dictator lies in a coma in a hospital in Panama, attended by doctor's sent from the US by President Eisenhower to his 'good neighbour', the regime arranges the transition of power to the dictator's two sons. Luis Somoza Debayle becomes dictator and Anastasio 'Tacho' Somoza Debayle head of the National Guard. **Tomás Borge** is imprisoned on suspicion of complicity.

1958

Jul 23 Large student demonstrations in León, in which Carlos Fonseca and other future Sandinista leaders are involved, against the visit of US functionary Milton Eisenhower to receive an honorary doctorate from the university.

¶–   General Ramón Raudales, a veteran of Sandino's army, falls in a guerrilla action, against the dictatorship, in the Yaule mountains.

1959

Jan   Cuban Revolution.

¶–   Carlos Fonseca and Silvio Mayorga organise the JDN (Nicaraguan Democratic Youth) to mobilise youth against the dictatorship.

Jun 24   Carlos Fonseca is seriously wounded in a guerrilla action at El Chaparral. A report (which turns out to be false) comes that he is dead and there are students protests in León.

Jul 23   JULY MASSACRE. Largest student demonstration in León, in which **Sergio Ramírez** and **Fernando Gordillo** take part. The Guard open-fires on the demonstrators and kills four students, wounding many more.

Aug   The journalist and revolutionary Manuel Díaz y Sotelo mounts a guerrilla action in the north. He is captured and later murdered.

1960

May 18   Edwin Castro, Ausberto Narváez and Cornelio Silva, imprisoned for complicity in the killing of Somoza, are murdered in prison by the National Guard.

¶–   **Sergio Ramírez** and **Fernando Gordillo** found the politically committed *Ventana* literary movement and magazine. They openly oppose the regime and the literary group calling themselves the 'Betrayed Generation', who condemn political commitment in the name of 'literary purity'.

1961

¶–   Carlos Fonseca, **Tomás Borge**, Silvio Mayorga, Enrique Lorente, Faustino Ruiz, **Fernando Gordillo**, Francisco Buitrago, Germán Pomares, Iván Sánchez, Santos López, Jorge Navarro, José Benito Escobar, Carlos Reyna, Rigoberto Cruz, Oscar Benavides, Eden Pastora and others set up the New Nicaragua Movement (MNN) . They denounce the US invasion of Cuba.

Apr   US invade Cuba at the Bay of Pigs, setting out from Puerto Cabezas in Nicaragua. They are defeated in just 72 hours.

Jul   FOUNDATION OF FSLN. At a meeting in Tegucigalpa Honduras, with **Tomás Borge** and Silvio Mayorga, Carlos

Fonseca proposes that the new revolutionary organisation should be called the Sandinista National Liberation Front (FSLN).

1962

¶– Carlos Fonseca and others explore the Río Coco area on the Northern border of Nicaragua in preparation for guerrilla action. Jorge Navarro intensifies the urban clandestine work of FSLN and publishes the clandestine paper *Trinchera*.

Oct Cuban missile crisis.

1963

Mar 22 FSLN squad takes over Radio Mundial in Managua and broadcasts a denunciation of President Kennedy's meeting with the Central American presidents.

May 31 FSLN action of 'economic recovery' raids the Bank of America in Managua to obtain funds.

Jul-Oct FIRST FSLN GUERRILLA ACTIONS INSIDE NICARAGUA. FSLN engage the National Guard in combat in the northern areas of the Río Coco and Bocay area. These actions give the FSLN their first public presence in the country. Jorge Navarro, Modesto Duarte, Iván Sánchez, Francisco Buitrago, Faustino Ruiz are killed.

1964

¶– Foundation of CONDECA, Co-ordinating Organisation of Central American Armies, representing US state department at regional level. FSLN intensifies work with peasants organised by Rigoberto Cruz ('Pablo Ubeda'), Carlos Reyna and others.

¶– Singer workers' strike.

Jun Carlos Fonseca is captured in Managua.

Aug US begins bombing Vietnam.

1965

Jan 2 Carlos Fonseca is deported to Guatemala.

Apr 40,000 US marines invade the Dominican Republic.

¶– US continues to bomb Vietnam.

¶– 40 kilometre march, led by Julio Buitrago and Francisco Moreno, to San Jacinto (where the Nicaraguans defeated the self-proclaimed president of Nicaragua, 'filibuster' William Walker, on 14th September 1856).

1966

¶– FSLN send Carlos Reyna as delegate to the Havana Tricontinental Conference of Solidarity with the Peoples of Asia, Africa and Latin America.

Feb 15 Camilo Torres, Colombian priest and guerrilla dies in combat in Colombia.

¶– Casimiro Sotelo and Julio Buitrago visit mining centres, denouncing workers' cruel exploitation by foreign monopolies.

Jul 23 National student day demonstration is celebrated for the first time on the campus of the Catholic University (UCA) in Managua. Casimiro Sotelo is expelled from the university. Demonstrations.

Jul FSLN militants Enrique Lorente and Selim Shible captured in Managua.

Oct FSLN 'economic recovery' raids on the La Criolla supermarket and a branch of the National Bank in Managua.

¶– Circulation of FSLN manifesto *Sandino yes, Somoza, no! Revolution yes, electoral farce no!*, signed by Carlos Fonseca, Silvio Mayorga, Rigoberto Cruz, Oscar Turcios and Conchita Alday (pseudonym of Doris Tijerino).

¶– **Ernesto Cardenal** and William Agudelo found their peasant community on the Solentiname Islands on Lake Nicaragua.

1967

Jan 20 FSLN attack a branch of the San Sebastián bank in an action of 'economic recovery'. Other bank raids follow during the year.

Jan 22 JANUARY MASSACRE. 60,000 join an electoral demonstration organised by the bourgeois opposition coalition party UNO. 500 demonstrators are killed by the Guard. The massacre destroys the credibility of the 'electoral farce' as a means of overthrowing the dictatorship.

Feb US navy bombs Vietnam.

Apr Che Guevara writes a letter from Bolivia to the Organisation of Solidarity with the Peoples of Asia, Africa and Latin America, insisting on the need to create 'one,

	two, many Vietnams' to destroy imperialism.
May 1	Concluding the 'electoral farce', the dictator Somoza reassumes the presidency of Nicaragua.
Aug 27	PANCASÁN. After months of organising a guerrilla base inside the country with peasant support, the FSLN is engaged in combat by the Guard at Pancasán and loses 13 senior members, including Silvio Mayorga, Rigoberto Cruz, Carlos Reyna, Oscar Danilo Rosales, Nicholas Sánchez and Francisco Moreno. This defeat becomes a political victory, as it focuses attention on the FSLN as the most credible opposition to the dictator.
¶–	The FSLN abandons *focismo* – armed uprisings by small guerrilla bases (*focos*) – as their main strategy. They expand their work among the peasantry and in towns. 1967-74 becomes a 'period of silent accumulation of forces'.
Nov 4	Casimiro Sotelo is captured with three other clandestine militants in daylight in the Monseñor Lezcano district of Managua, and assassinated in the dungeons of the Presidential Palace.
¶–	Latin American Bishops' Conference at Medellín proposes a 'preferential option for the poor'.
1968	
Sep 20	FSLN 'economic recovery' raid on the Bank of America in Managua.
¶–	Russell Tribunal condemns US war crimes in Vietnam.
1969	
¶–	Publication of the *Historic Programme of the FSLN*.
Apr	National Guard kills peasants in Yaosca associated with the Sandinista guerrillas.
Jul 15	DEATH OF JULIO BUITRAGO, leader of the FSLN forces in Managua, and a member of its directorate. His safe house near the Delicias del Volga in the Frixione district of Managua is detected by the Guard and besieged by 400 troops with machine guns and tear gas, backed up by aircraft and a Sherman tank. Julio resists to the end and dies singing the Sandinista Hymn. Fellow militant Doris Tijerino is captured when she manages to get a child out of the house. She is imprisoned and severely tortured. On

the same day, in the Santo Domingo district Alesio Blandón, Marco Antonio Rivera and Anibal Castrillo are captured in another safe house and killed.

Dec 23   Attempt by FSLN squad, led by Humberto Ortega, and including Germán Pomares ('El Danto'), to free Carlos Fonseca from jail in Costa Rica. The attempt fails and Humberto Ortega's arm is crippled.

1970

Jan 15   DEATH OF LEONEL RUGAMA. This poet, who had left the seminary to join the urban guerrillas in Managua, is detected in the safe house in the Cementerio Oriental district of Managua. The house is surrounded by troops, tanks and helicopters and **Leonel Rugama** dies hurling defiant insults at the Guard.

Apr 3   Luisa Amanda Espinosa, a domestic worker and clandestine messenger for the FSLN, is shot down crossing the Calle de Laborio in León. She is the FSLN's first woman militant martyr and has given her name to the Nicaraguan Women's organisation AMNLAE (Luisa Amanda Espinosa Nicaraguan Women's Association).

Oct 21   After an international campaign spearheaded by intellectuals including Roque Dalton (El Salvador) and Jean Paul Sartre and Simone de Beauvoir (France), for the release of Carlos Fonseca, a second successful action led by Carlos Agüero and involving a kidnapped Costa Rican plane, frees Fonseca, together with Humberto Ortega and others from jail and flies them to Mexico.

¶–   1970-72: Occupations of churches, schools and other buildings demanding the end of repression and release of prisoners.

1971

¶–   Political prisoners, backed by their mothers and supporters, go on hunger strike to protest at brutal treatment. Repression and protests continue. In the concentration camp at El Cuá many peasants are tortured and murdered. Some are flung alive from helicopters.

1972

Jan 23   EARTHQUAKE in Managua kills 10,000, injures a further 20,000 and leaves 300,000 homeless. Somoza appropriates the international relief for his own profit and uses it to extend his business empire. In particular, he invests in the hexagonal paving stones or large cobbles (*adoquines*) to pave many of the capital's streets. During the insurrection these will be uprooted and used as barricades – a particular pleasure for the revolutionaries.

1973

¶–   Building workers' strike, supported by students, health workers and other sectors.

Jul   Massive student action backing workers. Protests by banana workers on plantations controlled by Standard Fruit Company in Chinandega.

Sep 17   DEATH OF RICARDO MORALES. National Guard surprise FSLN safe house in Nandaime. Two women militants escape, guns in hand. **Ricardo Morales** and Oscar Turcios, both members of FSLN leadership, are killed, and also Jonathan González and Juan José Quezeda.

1974

Dec 27   RAID ON CHEMA CASTILLO'S CHRISTMAS PARTY. In an action which brings to an end the period of 'silent accumulation of forces', an FSLN squad led by Eduardo Contreras ('Comandante Marcos') raids a party given by Somoza's Minister of Agriculture, 'Chema' Castillo, for the dictator and US Ambassador Turner B. Shelton. FSLN hold the guests to ransom until their demands are met. These include publication of their statements in the press, a ransom of $1 million dollars, salary increases for groups of workers including common soldiers in the National Guard, and the release of political prisoners, among whom are **Daniel Ortega**, José Benito Escobar and **Carlos José Guadamuz**, who fly to Cuba. Somoza declares a 'state of siege' and 33 months of even fiercer repression ensue.

1975

¶–   FSLN SPLITS INTO 3 TENDENCIES. The Proletarian Tendency (TP) led by Jaime Wheelock, Luis Carrión and Carlos Nuñez, want to establish an orthodox Marxist party and concentrate on organisational work among the urban proletariat. The other two tendencies disagree with this as a single strategy on the grounds that the Nicaraguan urban working class is very small (20% of total labour force) and cannot provide the social base for a revolutionary movement. The Prolonged Popular War Tendency (GPP), led by **Tomás Borge**, Henry Ruiz and Bayardo Arce, insist on the rural campaign of attrition against the Guard on the model of Vietnam. Like the GPP, the Third – (*Tercerista*) – or Insurrectional Tendency, led by the brothers Humberto and **Daniel Ortega** and Victor Tirado, want multi-class alliances, but also insist on the potential for an insurrection to overthrow the regime.

Nov   Carlos Fonseca publishes *Summary of some Current Problems* and returns to Nicaragua to try and settle the dispute.

1976

Nov 7   Eduardo Contreras ('Comandante Marcos') is killed in an engagement on the Managua-León road.

Nov 8   DEATH OF CARLOS FONSECA. He is killed in a confrontation with the Guard in Zinica.

1977

Sep   Somoza lifts the state of siege under pressure from the bourgeois opposition.

¶–   Establishment of the women's organisation AMPRONAC.

¶-   Strike by sugar workers, which will lead to the establishment of the rural workers' union ATC in March 1978. The strike is supported by the agitational efforts of the FSLN Proletarian Tendency.

Oct   OCTOBER OFFENSIVE. *Tercerista* FSLN squads – not wanting the bourgeois opposition to gain ascendancy – attack the Guard in San Carlos (with militants from the Solentiname community), Ocotal and Masaya. Lack of coordination between the tendencies, with the GPP unaware of the plan for attack, exposes them to ambush by the Guard on the Masaya-Tipitapa road, in which GPP leader Pedro Arauz ('Comandante Federico') is killed on October 17th. Despite such muddles, the October Offensive convinces many Nicaraguans it is possible to take on the National Guard.

Nov   STATEMENT BY 'THE TWELVE'. *La Prensa* publishes a statement by *Los Doce* ('The Twelve'), supporting the FSLN. They are a group of twelve prominent professionals, none of whom is a politician, including writer **Sergio Ramírez**, two priests Fernando Cardenal and Miguel D'Escoto, banker Arturo Cruz. Their statement removes the FSLN's 'extremist' image, that has deterred some support.

1978

Jan 10   ASSASSINATION OF PEDRO JOAQUÍN CHAMORRO, editor of *La Prensa* and leader of conservative opposition party (UDEL), probably at the instigation of the dictator's son 'Tachito' Somoza, head of the National Guard. 50,000 demonstrate at Chamorro's funeral.

Feb 2   FSLN attack Rivas and Granada garrisons. The attack on Granada is led by Camilo Ortega.

Feb 19   UPRISING IN MONIMBÓ. The inhabitants of Monimbó, the Indian *barrio* of town Masaya, rise in a spontaneous protest.

Feb 26   Camilo Ortega, who has been sent with FSLN reinforcements for the uprising, is killed fighting the Guard in Las Sabogales, Masaya.

¶–   FSLN attack Rivas and Granada.

Mar 3   Uprising in Subtiava, Indian district of León.

Jul   *Los Doce* return to Nicaragua.

¶–   Establishment of the mass MPU (United Popular Movement) under FSLN leadership (includes the Socialist Party, 20 popular organisations, trade unions, students).

1978...

Aug 22 ASSAULT ON THE NATIONAL PALACE. *Tercerista* Rigoberto López Pérez squad, led by Eden Pastora ('Comandante Zero'), Hugo Torres ('Comandante Uno') and **Dora María Téllez** ('Comandante Dos'). The FSLN squad, disguised in National Guard uniforms of the elite EEBI counter-insurgency troop, take the National Palace and hold the deputies to ransom for 47 hours. Somoza is forced to agree to their demands, chief of which is the release of 85 political prisoners. The 58 (still alive) released, including **Tomás Borge**, Doris Tijerino and **Felipe Peña**, travel to the airport through huge cheering crowds and fly to Panama.

Aug 28 UPRISING IN MATAGALPA. Spontaneous insurrection in Matagalpa supported by resident Sandinistas.

Sep 9 SEPTEMBER INSURRECTION. Under FSLN leadership, uprisings follow in Estelí, Masaya and León. **Ernesto Castillo** is killed in the León insurrection.

Oct The bourgeois parties in the Broad Opposition Front (FAO) seek US support for '*Somocismo* without Somoza'. *Los Doce* withdraw from the talks.

1979

Jan Somoza announces continuation of his government until 1981 elections.

Feb COMMON FRONT AGAINST THE DICTATOR. Establishment under FSLN leadership of the National Patriotic Front, which unites the MPU, unions, *Los Doce*, PLI (Independent Liberals) and PPSC (Social Christian Party) in a common front against the dictatorship.

Mar 8 REUNIFICATION OF FSLN. Formal reunification statement of three FSLN tendencies.

Mar 27 Germán Pomares leads eighty combatants from all three tendencies to occupy El Jicaro.

Apr Insurrection in Estelí. FSLN led by Comandante Francisco Rivera ('El Zorro').

May 17 126-strong Jacinto Hernández column enter the country from Costa Rica and advance through Nueva Guinea in the south east of Nicaragua. They succeed in diverting massive Somozan forces to the region but are surprised

	and almost the whole column is wiped out.
May 24	Germán Pomares dies of wounds after leading the attack on Jinotega.
May 29	FINAL OFFENSIVE. 300 strong column of the 'Benjamin Zeledón' Southern Front cross the border from Costa Rica and attack Rivas.
¶–	Attack on all fronts to converge on Managua: the 'Carlos Fonseca' Northern Front concentrate on Estelí; the 'Rigoberto López Pérez' North Western Front: Chinandega and León; the 'Camilo Ortega' Internal Front: Masaya and Managua; the 'Roberto Huembes' Eastern Front: mining districts of Siuna. **Felipe Peña** is killed fighting with the Nueva Guinea Front.
May 31	FSLN call for an insurrection and general strike. They broadcast from 'somewhere in Nicaragua': 'Heroic people of Nicaragua the hour of the overthrow of the infamous dictatorship has come...'
Jun 2	FSLN enter León
Jun 4	GENERAL STRIKE begins. The response is massive.
Jun 4	FSLN TAKE LEÓN, the first city to be wholly liberated from the Guard.
Jun 9	Insurrection in Managua.
Jun 16	Provisional Junta of National Reconstruction is set up in Costa Rica: **Daniel Ortega** (FSLN), **Sergio Ramírez** (*Los Doce*), Moisés Hassan (MPU) and two members of the bourgeois opposition: Violeta Chamorro (UDEL, conservative opposition party founded by her husband Pedro Joaquín), Alfonso Robelo (MDN, representing business interests).
Jun 24	FSLN take the Guard barracks in Masaya.
Jun 27	FSLN order strategic retreat from Managua to Masaya. 6000 leave Managua secretly at night.
Jul 2	FSLN take Matagalpa.
Jul 16	FSLN take the Guard barracks in Estelí.
Jul 17	Somoza resigns and flies to Miami.
Jul 18	NEW GOVERNMENT INSTALLED. Government Junta of National Reconstruction is formally installed in León University, where many of the FSLN leaders began their revolutionary careers.

1979...

Jul 19   TRIUMPH OF THE REVOLUTION. FSLN ENTER MANAGUA. FSLN forces from all Fronts converge on Managua and are welcomed by crowds of 250,000 people.

Jul 20   Government Junta of National Reconstruction and the FSLN leadership arrive in Managua, with huge crowds still celebrating the Triumph of the Revolution.

Jul   Immediately after the triumph the country is run through the renamed Sandinista Defence Committees (CDS), who oversee food distribution, housing, care of orphans etc.

¶–   MINISTRY OF THE INTERIOR. **Tomás Borge** becomes Minister of the Interior and head of state security.

July 20   DECREE CONFISCATES ALL SOMOZA'S LAND. By the end of 1979, 800,000 hectares, 20% of all cultivable land, is state-owned. Co-operatives are established and credit for farming.

Aug 8   UNIFIED NATIONAL HEALTH SERVICE is set up aiming to offer free and universal health care. The new Ministry of Health (MINSA) builds new hospitals, clinics and health posts and mounts vaccination campaigns to eliminate dangerous infectious diseases. Polio and diphtheria are eliminated by 1983. **Dora María Téllez** becomes Minister of Health.

Aug 22   FUNDAMENTAL STATUTE OF THE REPUBLIC abolishes the *Somocista* state.

Aug   Establishment of AMNLAE Women's Organisation.

Aug   MINISTRY OF EDUCATION under Fernando Cardenal is set up to provide free public education (between 1978 and 1987 enrolment in education programmes increases by 96%). They prepare for the 1980 literacy crusade.

Sep 2   Creation of EPS (Sandinista People's Army).

Sep   At the Havana summit Nicaragua joins the Non-Aligned Movement.

Sep   MINISTRY OF HOUSING law gives security of tenure to 50,000 family homes and punishes exploitative developers.

Sep   MINISTRY OF CULTURE establishes its first poetry workshop in Monimbó, and shortly afterwards in Subtiava. By 1982 at least 66 workshops meet regularly throughout the country. The Ministry will publish the prestigious journal *Nicaráuac* and the popular magazine *Poesía Libre*. It runs an annual Poetry Marathon in Ciudad Darío till 1988. The Minister of Culture is **Ernesto Cardenal**.

1980

¶–   Price controls for basic goods.

Jan   Rental law gives tenants security of their homes and controls rents at a low level.

¶–   New Government accepts Nicaragua's foreign debt, including that incurred by Somoza for repression. They hope this will help them obtain Western aid and credit from capitalist organisations but this is increasingly blocked by the US.

Feb   FORMATION OF POPULAR MILITIAS. Voluntary militia forces (MPS) are set up for national defence.

Apr   Violeta Chamorro resigns from the Junta for 'health reasons'. Alfonso Robelo resigns from the Junta.

Mar 10   The FSLN newspaper *Barricada* publishes Ernesto Cardenal's 'Rules' for writing poetry.

Mar-Aug   LITERACY CRUSADE. 100,000 young *brigadistas* teach literacy throughout the country. On the Atlantic coast Indian peoples are taught to read in their own languages. 56 teachers die in the campaign, which reduces illiteracy from over 50% to 12.9% and wins a UNESCO prize. After the literacy crusade Popular Education Collectives (CEPs) are set up to consolidate adult education.

May 4   COUNCIL OF STATE is set up to govern with the Junta. The Council has 47 members representing the various social sectors and popular organisations. Archbishop Obando y Bravo is president.

Nov   Alfonso Robelo organises MDN demonstration against 'totalitarianism'. Large Sandinista crowds resist the demonstrators and sack MDN offices.

1981

Jan REAGAN BECOMES US PRESIDENT and funds CIA counter-revolutionary activities. From 1981 onwards Nicaragua is in danger of a direct US invasion to overthrow the Sandinista government.

Mar Debate about the literary merit of poetry from the workshops in *Ventana*, the cultural supplement of *Barricada*. **Rosario Murillo** and **Gioconda Belli** criticise, **José Coronel Urtecho** defends and the workshop poets defend themselves.

Mar CONTRA MILITARY FORCE IS SET UP. The Nicaraguan Democratic Forces (FDN) consisting mainly of ex-National Guardsmen is established, with US government support operating through the CIA. (Later, via various routes, this Contra group is joined by Alfredo César, Arturo Cruz and Alfonso Robelo). They specialise in attacks on clinics, schools and co-ops.

Apr Foundation of UNAG (National Union of Farmers and Cattle Breeders) representing small and middle level farmers, who feel their interests are not represented in ATC (the agricultural workers' union).

Apr Reagan administration cuts off all aid to Nicaragua.

May 2 **Ernesto Cardenal** gives the closing speech at Harvard Congress on Disarmament and Peace. He says Nicaragua's poets are ready to fight to defend their revolution but also hope one day arms will not be necessary. He concludes: 'We can advise other armies – on matters of poetry'.

Jul FIRST ISSUE OF *POESÍA LIBRE*, edited by **Julio Valle-Castillo**, contains 'Song of the Nicaraguas' (the first extant Nicaraguan poem), three unpublished poems by **Leonel Rugama**, poems from the workshops and some Palestinian combat poetry.

Jul 19 AGRARIAN REFORM LAW confiscates unused large estates (making total confiscated land 40%). Some land is used for state farms and co-operatives and, in response to demands by UNAG, some land is distributed as individual plots to small farmers.

¶– Popular Health Days are established, using health

brigadistas for public health education and vaccination campaigns.

Sep   Law abolishing *Patria Potestad* gives women equal rights over their children.

Nov   The Reagan administration authorises $20 million to destabilise the Nicaraguan government.

Dec   FIRST POETRY WORKSHOPS CONFERENCE. Mayra Jiménez says the number of poetry workshops far exceeds the original plan. Co-ordinators of the workshops are: **Carlos Calero** (Monimbó), **Cony Pacheco** (Subtiava), **Juan Ramón Falcón** (Condega), **Gerardo Gadea** (EPS).

1982

Jan   Increased Contra activity on the Atlantic coast leads the Nicaraguan government to relocate Miskito Indian communities from the Río Coco further inland. 10,000 Miskitos flee to Honduras.

Feb 20   Contras bomb Managua airport killing 3.

Mar   Contras bomb two key bridges in the North.

Apr   **Ernesto Cardenal** speaks to UNESCO: 'Nicaragua's cultural liberation has been part of the national liberation struggle'.

Sep   Eden Pastora and Alfonso Robelo set up Contra force ARDE in Costa Rica.

Nov   US Congress approves $24 million in covert aid to the Contras.

1983

Jan   Contadora Group is formed by Venezuela, Colombia, Mexico and Panama to seek a peaceful solution to the Central American conflicts.

Feb   Over 5,000 US and Honduran troops take part in the 'Big Pine' military manoeuvres 10 miles from the Nicaraguan border. Further exercises follow in August.

Mar   POPE PAUL II VISITS NICARAGUA. He insults mothers whose children have just been killed by the Contra. He insults **Ernesto Cardenal**, Minister of Culture and one of 3 catholic priests in the Sandinista government.

Jun   US closes Nicaraguan consulates. Nicaragua responds by abolishing visa requirement for US citizens. US Treasury Department announces official policy of opposing all

	multilateral loans to Nicaragua.
Aug	Conscription is introduced for national defence, which is condemned by the Catholic Church.
Oct	CIA-trained saboteurs attack Nicaragua's largest port, Corinto, and destroy precious oil reserves.
Oct	US invades Grenada.

1984

¶–	From 1984 to 1988 50% of Nicaragua's budget is spent on defence.
Jan	Contadora initiative drafts a Central American Peace plan, aiming to reduce militarisation in the area. The plan is sabotaged by US, because the plan acknowledges the legitimacy of the Sandinista government, and demands withdrawal of US troops from Honduras and an end to US military spending in the region.
Feb-Mar	US MINES NICARAGUA'S PORTS.
May	International Court at The Hague orders US to stop mining Nicaraguan ports.
Nov 4	ELECTIONS.. **Daniel Ortega** is elected President and **Sergio Ramírez** Vice President with 67% of votes. FSLN win a majority in National Assembly with 64% of seats. Arturo Cruz representing rightwing MDN withdraws at the last minute. Observers from many countries declare the elections are fair but US refuses to recognise them.
Nov	US elections. Reagan is re-elected President.

1985

May 1	US DECLARES TOTAL TRADE EMBARGO ON NICARAGUA.
Jun	US Congress approves $27 million in 'humanitarian aid' to the Contras.
¶–	The Nicaraguan government apologises to the Miskito Indians and allows them to return to the Río Coco.
¶–	Obando y Bravo is made a cardinal, the only one in Central America.

1986

Apr	US air force bombs Libya, taking off from Lakenheath Base in East Anglia.
May	ARDE, the main Contra group on Nicaragua's southern border, disintegrates.
Jun	US CONGRESS VOTES $100 MILLION AID TO THE CONTRAS,

including military aid.

¶– Sandinistas shut down pro-Contra Radio Católica and the opposition daily newspaper *La Prensa*. Two church officials critical of the government are expelled.

Jun INTERNATIONAL COURT AT THE HAGUE CONDEMNS US aggression against Nicaragua and enters provisional judgment for $17 billion damages against US.

Oct 5 Sandinista troops shoot down a C-123 cargo plane capturing US marine Eugene Hasenfus, who says he is part of a CIA arms delivery operation to the Contras. Hasenfus, sentenced to 30 years in prison, is released after one month on humanitarian grounds by the Nicaraguan government.

Nov Iran-Contra scandal breaks in Washington and embarrasses US government.

1987

Jan 9 PROMULGATION OF NEW NICARAGUAN CONSTITUTION after many consultations.

Feb First draft of Central American Peace Plan, named the Arias Peace Plan after the President of Costa Rica, demands immediate elections in Nicaragua and direct talks with the Contras. Nicaragua is excluded from its launch and rejects the plan.

¶– Second draft of the Peace Plan no longer requires immediate elections or direct talks with Contras. It calls on governments to cut off aid to all irregular forces in the region. Nicaragua accepts.

¶– INCREASING ECONOMIC CRISIS. High inflation. Huge cost of war and economic aggression together with increasing foreign debt leads to a fall in living standards and attrition of social gains of the revolution.

¶– Human cost of the war between 1980 and June 1987: 50,000 killed, wounded or abducted, of whom 22,495 killed i.e. 0.6% of population. 250,000 displaced from their homes. Contra specialise in attacking revolutionary installations and civilian targets: health posts, schools, co-ops.

1987...

Jul 19   **Daniel Ortega** makes a speech calculating US has invested US$15.6 billion in trying to destroy the Revolution.

Aug   PEACE PLAN IS SIGNED.. After disagreements with the US, the third draft of the Arias Peace Plan is finally signed. It provides for ceasefire agreements, an end to states of emergency and an end to aid from governments to all irregular or insurrectional forces in the region.

Sep   Autonomy Law for the Atlantic Coast.

Sep-Dec   Nicaragua enacts provisions of the Arias peace accords. *La Prensa* and Radio Católica are allowed to resume production. A unilateral ceasefire is declared.

1988

Feb   WORSENING ECONOMY leads the Nicaraguan government to impose monetarist measures, cutting public expenditure and credits, sacking public employees, lifting price controls. Devaluation leads to hyperinflation. Wages of many workers fall below subsistence levels. Fall in 'social wage'. US have succeeded in their declared policy of 'making the Nicaraguan economy scream'.

Mar   Nicaraguan government and Contra representatives meet at Sapóa, and agree to a provisional ceasefire. Subsequent negotiations break down due to excessive Contra demands and US hostility to the agreement.

Oct 22   HURRICANE JOAN causes havoc, particularly along the Atlantic Coast. Many are killed and the damage is estimated at $840 million.

Nov   George Bush, ex-CIA director, is elected US president. Bush declares his continued support for Contras.

¶–   INFLATION RISES. By the end of 1988 inflation in Nicaragua reaches over 30,000%.

1989

¶–   Nicaraguan government imposes a further round of spending cuts and redundancies.

Feb   Central American presidents meet and reach an agreement on Contra demobilisation. Nicaragua announces 1990 elections are to be held in February.

Mar   US Congress approves $50 million in 'non-lethal' aid to

	keep the Contras intact.
Aug	Central American leaders agree to December deadline for Contra demobilisation under international supervision by UN and the Organisation of American States (OAS).
Oct	US Congress votes $9 million for UNO election campaign. $5 million additional covert assistance is promised by CIA.
Dec	Contras ignore the demobilisation deadline.

1990

| Feb 25 | ELECTIONS, won by US-backed UNO coalition of 14 parties ranging from conservatives to communists. Violeta Chamorro becomes President and far-right Virgilio Godoy becomes her Vice President, with 55% of the vote. In the presidential election FSLN gets 41% of the vote. In the National Assembly UNO gets 51 seats, FSLN gets 39, out of a total of 92. |

NOTES

The translator apologises to the poets for the shortcomings in these notes, especially to those whose notes are short.

The notes are in alphabetical order of surnames with notes on the poems under the poet's name. Anon is listed alphabetically under Anon.

Many of the songs mentioned in these notes are available on cassette from the Nicaragua Solidarity Campaign, Red Rose Club, 129 Seven Sisters Road, London N7 (071 272 9619).

ABBREVIATIONS

ENN: Editorial Nueva Nicaragua, the publishing house set up after the Revolution which published large quantities of poetry.

PPN: *Poesía política nicaragüense*, an anthology of Nicaraguan political verse edited by Francisco de Asís Fernández (Ministry of Culture, Managua 1986).

NICARAGUAN WORDS IN THE POEMS

Brigadista: Brigade member (here, usually literacy brigade)
Compañero/a: comrade
Compa: comrade (short familiar form)
Frente: (Sandinista) Front
Guerrillero/a: Guerrilla combatant
Tamales: Nicaraguan pasty or cake, made with maize dough, which may be stuffed, and cooked wrapped in a plantain leaf.

A few birds have kept their Nicaraguan names. Popular Nicaraguan bird names are often onomatopoeic.

THE POETS

Luz Marina Acosta   Pages: 144-9

Sandinista *guerrillera*. She worked with Ernesto Cardenal in the Ministry of Culture and now works in his office in the Casa de los Tres Mundos. Her poems have been published in *Poesía Libre* and *Nuevo Amanecer Cultural*.

How can I write a love poem?   Pages: 148-9

This poem was published in *Poesía Libre* 16. The Ministry of Culture was set up in El Retiro, a fine house and garden near the Plaza España in Managua, which had belonged to Somoza.

Anon: Song of the Nicaraguas   Pages: 234-5

This is the first extant Nicaraguan poem written in Nahuatl in the sixteenth century at the beginning of the long night of the Spanish conquest. It was translated into Spanish by the great Mexican Nahuatl scholar Angel María Garibay. It was published on page 1 of issue 1 of *Poesía Libre*, the Sandinista Ministry of Culture's poetry magazine.

Gioconda Belli   Pages: 194-209

Born 1948, she joined the FSLN in 1970, recruited by Camilo Ortega. In 1974 she published her first collection *Sobre la grama*. She was part of the support team for the FSLN raid on the dictator's friend Chema Castillo's Christmas party, on December 27th 1974, after which she went into exile. Her novel *La mujer habitada* (Vanguardia, Managua 1988) gives a fictionalised account of this action. In exile she published her first explicitly political collection, *Linea de Fuego* (Casa de las Americas, Havana 1978), which won the Casa de las Americas prize. After the Revolution she worked with the newly set up Women's Association AMNLAE (Luisa Amanda Espinosa Association of Nicaraguan Women). Since 1979 she has published two poetry collections: *Trueno y arcoiris* (ENN, Managua 1982) and *De la costilla de Eva* (ENN, Managua 1986). The three poems translated here are from the latter, which also contains her poem 'No pasarán', which was set to music by Carlos Mejía Godoy and became one of Nicaragua's most famous revolutionary songs. Her collected works to date appeared as *El ojo de la mujer* (Vanguardia, Managua 1991). Some of her poems are translated into English in the pamphlet *Nicaragua Water Fire* (trans. John Lyons, Greville Press, Warwick 1989) and in *Lovers and Comrades* (ed. Amanda Hopkinson, Women's Press, London 1989)

It Happened one Sunday on a Trip to the Beach   Pages: 194-7

The poem is dated 1986. For Ricardo Morales, see below and his poems on pages 62-71.

We Shall Go On Being Born   Pages: 198-201

The National Palace, along one side of the Plaza de la Revolución in Managua, has a large picture of Carlos Fonseca on it.

Nicaragua Water Fire   Pages: 202-9

'There goes the General': 'Allá va el General' is a well-known song about Sandino by Luis Enrique Mejía Godoy.

La Prensa: the anti-Sandinista paper, comes out in the afternoon.

The flame tree, also called 'flamboyant' (Nicaraguan: *malinche*; Latin: *delonix regia*) has bright red flowers followed by large rattling pods shaped like machetes. Malinche was the name of a high-born Indian lady who became the mistress of the conquistador Cortés and betrayed her people. Nicaraguan readers of the poem would appreciate the contrast with the heroic fighter in the poem.

Martha Blandino

During the Literacy Campaign she taught in Los Pocitos. The literacy campaign from March to August 1980, directed by Sandinista Minister of Education Fernando Cardenal, Ernesto's brother, reduced illiteracy from nearly 60% to 12% and won a UNESCO prize. The campaign also recovered some of the country's cultural riches. The young literacy teachers who went out to teach people to read and write also learnt what they could from their pupils. 'Among other things we collected the oral history of the national liberation war, names of flora and fauna, typical dishes, medicinal herbs, archaeological sites, and those with mineral deposits, handicrafts, myths, legends and popular songs'. And as Martha says in her poem, the literacy campaign was the first taste of country living for many urban young people. The poem appears in *Fogata en la Oscurana*, an anthology of poems by literacy workers (Ministry of Culture, Managua 1985).

Tomás Borge

Born 1930 in Matagalpa, he studied at León University and was imprisoned for complicity after Rigoberto López Pérez killed the dictator Somoza García in 1956. In 1961 he co-founded the FSLN with Carlos Fonseca and Silvio Mayorga – he is the only founder still alive. He was captured in Managua after leaving a secret meeting in the Colonia Centroamérica, on Feb 4th 1976. When arrested he shouted out his name very loudly and said he was sure this saved him from being murdered in prison. In prison he wrote poems and, after hearing of the death of Carlos Fonseca on November 8th 1976, he wrote a memoir of him *Carlos el amanecer ya no es una tentación* (to be published by Katabasis in Tomás Borge and others, *Carlos Fonseca*). He was released with 58 other political prisoners on 23 August 1978 through the Sandinista Assault on the National Palace. After the triumph of the Revolution he became Minister of the Interior. He has published an autobiographical memoir *La paciente impaciencia* (Vanguardia, Managua 1989): *The Patient Impatience* (Curbstone Press, Wilmantic USA 1992) and his poems are collected in *La Ceremonia esperada* (ENN, Managua 1990), from which the three poems translated here are taken.

Letter to Ana Josefina   Pages: 72-81

In *The Patient Impatience* Tomás relates how he risked his life coming out of hiding to visit the hospital in Diriamba when Ana Josefina was born. Guards surrounded the hospital in search of him but he managed to escape. His wife Josefina brought the baby to visit him in prison.

Prison Visit   Pages: 82-5

Describes a visit by Tomás' wife Josefina.

Carlos Calero   Pages: 178-81

A carpenter born in Masaya, he studied literature at the UNAN (National Autonomous University) in Managua. He took part in the Literacy Campaign and was a militia member. One of the organisers of the poetry workshops and on the editorial board of *Poesía Libre* representing Monimbó. His poems appear in the anthologies *Talleres de Poesía* (Ministry of Culture, 1983: from which the poem here is taken) and *Fogata en la Oscurana* (1985).

Ernesto Cardenal   Pages: 20-1, 28-9, 106-123, 236-9

Born in 1925 into a conservative family in Granada, he studied in Mexico (1943-7) and Columbia University, New York (1947-9). After a religious conversion in 1956 he entered the Trappist Monastery in Kentucky, where Thomas Merton was novice master, moving on to the Benedictine monastery at Cuernavaca, Mexico and La Ceja, Colombia. Ordained in 1965, he set up a community composed mainly of peasants in the Solentiname islands on Lake Nicaragua. He was deeply impressed by the Cuban Revolution during a visit in 1970 and his next long poem *Canto Nacional* (1972) was dedicated to the FSLN. After the Managua earthquake he wrote another long documentary poem, *Oráculo sobre Managua* (1973), containing a graphic account of Leonel Rugama's death fighting the Guard. In 1976 he invited Mayra Jiménez to Solentiname to establish the first poetry workshop. The Solentiname community, including most of the members of the poetry workshop, took part in the assault on San Carlos barracks on 13th October 1977. In retaliation, the National Guard smashed the community. Cardenal went into exile, becoming a roving ambassador for the FSLN. With the triumph of the Revolution he became Minister of Culture. Poetry workshops were set up all over the country and he published some 'Rules' for aspiring poets. His most recent poem – 581 pages long – is *Cántico Cósmico* (ENN, Managua 1989). His works have been widely translated and among those published in Britain are *Love* (trans. DL, Search Press, London 1974); *Prayer for Marilyn Monroe and other Poems* (trans. Robert Pring-Mill, Search Press, London 1975); *Psalms* (trans. John Heath-Stubbs and others, Sheed and Ward, London 1981); *Nicaraguan New Time* (trans. DL, Journeyman, London 1988); *The Music of the Spheres* (trans. DL, Katabasis, London 1990).

Epitaph for the Tomb of Adolfo Báez Bone   Pages: 20-1

Originally written for Sandino and called 'En la tumba del guerrillero' ('The Guerrilla's Tomb'), the poem was published (in 1961 in *Epigramas*)) for his friend Adolfo Báez Bone, who was killed in the 1954 April conspiracy to capture the dictator. When the conspiracy failed, Cardenal, who took part in it, had to go into hiding. Cardenal regarded this as his first successful political poem and some years later Carlos Mejía Godoy made it into a song. One of the cantos of Cardenal's poem 'Zero Hour' is about the April conspiracy.

The Pork that Rigoberto Did not Eat   Pages: 28-9

was published in *Vuelos de Victoria* (UNAN, León 1985), as were the five poems by Cardenal in the text of the anthology.

Final Offensive   Pages: 110-3

The FSLN Final Offensive began in May 1979. At the end of the poem there is a reference to Leonel Rugama's poem,'The Earth is a Satellite of the Moon' (see page 52).

To Ernesto Castillo, my Nephew Pages: 114-5

The poem expresses very concretely how Cardenal had abandoned the pacifist position of his former novice master Thomas Merton and come to agree with Leonel Rugama that there was 'no alternative but the struggle'. For Ernesto Castillo, see below and his poems on pages 102-5.

Cabinet Meeting Pages: 116-9

Poets in this anthology besides Ernesto Cardenal who were in the Sandinista government: Daniel Ortega, President; Sergio Ramírez, Vice President; Tomás Borge, Minister of the Interior; Dora María Téllez, Minister of Health. Daisy Zamora was Vice Minister of Culture.

Waslala Pages: 120-3

Cardenal's two poems 'The Peasant Women of Cuá' and 'The Arrival of the Women of Cuá' (translated in *Nicaraguan New Time*, London 1988), which were also made into a song by Carlos Mejía Godoy, relate how these women would not tell where the guerrillas were and their cries under torture were 'gritos de parto': cries of the country in labour.

The Guerrilla's Tomb Pages: 236-9

This poem is also in *Vuelos de Victoria*. It takes over the original title of the 'Epitaph for Adolfo Baéz Bone'. Much of Cardenal's poetry, (for example, *The Music of the Spheres*) expresses his fascination with flying, the sky, planets, stars and other cosmic matters.

Ernesto Castillo Pages: 102-5

Born 1957, he studied in Barcelona and Costa Rica, where he joined the FSLN, supplying arms and information. Aged 20, he took part in the León insurrection. On the night of September 9th 1978, while he was urging his comrades to advance and shouting 'Patria libre o morir!' ('A free country or death!'), he was shot in the head and killed by a sharpshooter. His poems were found after his death and published as *Antología póstuma*. His uncle, Ernesto Cardenal, wrote a poem about him (see pages 114-5).

Bosco Centeno   Pages: 152-9

Born in 1953, he was a member of Ernesto Cardenal's peasant community in Solentiname and took part in the Assault on San Carlos on October 13th 1977, after which he became an FSLN combatant on the Southern Front. With the triumph of the Revolution he became a captain in the EPS (Sandinista People's Army). Bosco Centeno, together with two other poets in this anthology, Iván Guevara and Felipe Peña, contributed to *El asalto a San Carlos. Testimonios de Solentiname* (Ministry of Culture, Managua 1986). The poems translated here appear in *Puyonearon los granos* (Ministry of Culture, 1984), which won the Leonel Rugama prize for young poets. His poems also appear in the anthology *Poesia campesina de Solentiname* (Ministry of Culture, 1985). More of his poems are translated in *The Peasant Poets of Solentiname* (trans. Peter Wright, Katabasis, London 1991).

To Elvis Chavarría   Pages: 154-5

Elvis Chavarría was a fellow member of the Solentiname community, who was killed in the Assault on San Carlos on 13th October 1977. The Father is Ernesto Cardenal.

Juan Ramón Falcón   Pages: 170-77

Born in Condega into a peasant family, he studied engineering at night school, became a poet and primitive painter. He was one of the organisers of the poetry workshops and on the editorial board of *Poesía Libre*, representing Condega. Together with some of the other organisers he belonged to the Ernesto Castillo poetry workshop in Managua. He was a militia member and also regularly went to help with the coffee harvest. His poems appear in *Poesía Libre* and the anthology *Talleres de Poesía* (1983).

Lorena Faber 'Linda'   Pages: 170-1

'Linda' would be her pseudonym as an FSLN militant.

Mayra: Mayra Jiménez, the Costa Rican poet invited by Ernesto Cardenal to set up the first poetry workshop in Solentiname in 1976, and to set up poetry workshops all over the country after the Revolution.

Letter Poem for Ninfa Vélez 'Diana'   Pages: 172-77

'Diana' would be her pseudonym as an FSLN militant.

Ernesto Castillo: see above and his poems on pages 102-5.

Camilo Torres: Colombian guerrilla priest who was killed fighting in Colombia in February 1966.

José Benito Escobar: Member of FSLN National Directorate. Born of working class parents in 1936, he was an activist in the construction workers' strike of 1958. In 1960 he co-founded the JRN (Nicaraguan Revolutionary Youth) and in 1960 the MNN (New Nicaragua Movement), the direct predecessor to the FSLN. He was murdered by the National Guard in Estelí on July 16th 1978. There is a song about him, 'Usted compañero', in the *Canto Epico* translated in *The Nicaraguan Epic* (Katabasis, London 1989).

Gerardo Gadea   Pages: 182-5

Born in León, FSLN combatant. After the Triumph he became a political officer in the EPS (Sandinista People's Army), whom he represented on the editorial board of *Poesía Libre*. He belonged to the Ernesto Castillo poetry workshop in Managua. His poems appear in the anthologies *Talleres de Poesía* (1983) and *Poesía de las Fuerzas Armadas* (1985: both Ministry of Culture). The poem translated here is from the latter anthology.

In the Military School Pages: 182-5

Bugle-bird: *Zanate clarinero* (Latin: *quiscalus macrourus*), also known as a 'grackle' in English, is a very common Nicaraguan bird rather like a starling. The male is a brilliant blue-black and is known as 'clarinero' ('bugler') because its strident song sounds like a bugle.

Flame tree: *malinche* (Latin: *Delonix regia*), also known as a 'flamboyant' in English, has brilliant scarlet flowers in May, which only last a short time, to be followed by long machete-shaped pods for the rest of the year.

Winter: There are two seasons in Nicaragua, hot and dry called summer and hot and wet called winter. The winter season begins with rains in May after the long drought.

Germán Pomares Ordoñez: Sandinista leader from early days known as 'El Danto' ('The Tapir'). On March 27th 1979 he led eighty guerrillas, from the reunited three tendencies of the FSLN, to occupy El Jicaro. He died on May 24th 1979 leading the attack on Jinotega.

Carlos Fonseca Amador: One of the founders of the FSLN in 1961. He became FSLN commander in chief. He was killed in the mountains of Zinica on November 8th 1976. After the Triumph he was ceremonially re-buried in the Plaza de la Revolución in Managua and a memorial built with a constantly burning flame. This was extinguished after the Sandinista defeat in 1990 and in November 1991 there was a right-wing bomb attack on his tomb. Tomás Borge's account of his life *Carlos the Dawn is no longer in Doubt* will be published by Katabasis in Tomás Borge and others, *Carlos Fonseca*.

Carlos Agüero: Sandinista guerrilla who on December 23rd 1969 led the successful spectacular attempt, involving a kidnapped Costa Rican plane, to free Carlos Fonseca, Humberto Ortega and others from jail in Costa Rica. Agüero accompanied Carlos Fonseca on his final clandestine trip through Nicaragua in 1976 and was with him at his death. Carlos Agüero fell in combat at Lisawé, Zelaya on 7th April 1977.

'Together with the militia recruits': In this military school, some were training for the professional army, the EPS (Sandinista People's Army). Those in the militias (MPS: Popular Sandinista Militias) were volunteers.

Ana Ilce Gómez   Pages: 32-3

Born Masaya 1945, she studied journalism at the National University of Nicaragua. Her poems began to appear in the sixties but she did not belong to any of the literary groups. 'The Hidden Limits' is from her collection *Las ceremonias del silencio* (El Pez y la serpiente, Managua 1975; re-issued by Vanguardia, Managua 1989). There is a selection of her poems in *La mujer nicaragüenese en la poesía* (ed. Daisy Zamora, ENN, Managua 1992). Some of her poems are translated in *Lovers and Comrades* (London 1989).

Fernando Gordillo   Pages: 36-7

Born 1940, he studied law at León University, where he was active in the FER (Revolutionary Student Front), the cradle of many future FSLN militants. He took part in the student demonstration of 23rd July 1959 in León, in which four students were killed by the Guard. With fellow law student Sergio Ramírez he co-founded the *Frente Ventana*, which published a committed literary magazine and opposed the 'art for art's sake' literary group calling itself the 'Betrayed Generation'. Michèle Najlis, who describes herself as the 'younger sister' in the *Ventana* group, became Gordillo's *compañera*. Gordillo, a highly esteemed intellectual in the young revolutionary movement, fell ill with the disease *miastenia gravis* in 1961, which confined him to a wheel chair and killed in him 1967. The poem translated here appears in Fernando Gordillo, *Obras* (ENN, Managua 1989) and in PPN.

A Country's Price   Pages: 36-7

By the Bryan–Chamorro Treaty (signed 1914, ratified 1916) 'the Government of Nicaragua grants in perpetuity to the government of the United States, forever free from all taxation or other public charge, the exclusive property rights necessary and convenient for the construction, operation and maintenance of an inter-oceanic canal.' In return the US government paid $3 million, all of which passed directly to US banks holding the Nicaraguan debt. 3 million is also about the population of Nicaragua. The words 'the highest of songs is the struggle' became the motto of Carlos Mejía Godoy's group of revolutionary singers *Los de Palacaguïna*.

Carlos José Guadamuz   Pages: 50-1

Born 1945, he joined the FSLN in 1963. Imprisoned in 1969, he spent time in prison with Daniel Ortega, José Benito Escobar and other FSLN militants. They were released through the FSLN action of 27th December 1974. He is interviewed, as well as a number of other Nicaraguan writers, by Margaret Randall in *Risking a Somersault in the Air* (San Francisco 1984). After the triumph of the Revolution he ran the state radio station Radio Voz de Nicaragua. His book *Y las casas se quedaron llenas de humo* (ENN, Managua 1982) – whose title is taken from Leonel Rugama's poem translated on pages 52-5 – contains a prose memoir and some poems, including the poem translated here. He also has poems in PPN.

Iván Guevara   Pages: 160-1

A member of Ernesto Cardenal's peasant community in Solentiname, he took part in the Assault on San Carlos Barracks on October 13th 1977. After the Revolution he became a captain in the EPS (Sandinista People's Army). His poems are published in *Poesía campesina de Solentiname* and *Poesía de las fuerzas armadas* (both Ministry of Culture 1985). The poem translated here is from the latter collection. A further selection of his poems are translated in *The Peasant Poets of Solentiname* (trans. Peter Wright, London 1991).

Rigoberto López Pérez   Pages: 22-7

Born 1930, he studied in the University of León. He executed the dictator Somoza García on 21st September 1956 at a party in León. He himself was shot dead immediately afterwards.

Last Letter to his Mother, extract   Pages: 22-7

This extract from the letter was set out in lines of verse, with the irregular indentations also favoured by Ernesto Cardenal, by Carlos Fonseca. In the rest of the letter Rigoberto tells his mother he has taken out some life insurance for her in case he is killed. The poem is published in PPN.

David Macfield   Pages: 150-1

A black poet, born 1936 in Ciudad Rama on the Nicaraguan Atlantic Coast, and also a songwriter and musician. For five years he was a shoe-shiner and for two years a fruit seller on the Atlantic Coast. During the seventies he became a member of the *Gradas* cultural group, to whom Rosario Murillo and Carlos Mejía Godoy also belonged. His collection *Las Veinticuatro – Poemas y Canciones* (Libromundo, Managua 1975) contains poems and also the texts of his famous songs such as 'Pancasán' and 'Nació el niño negro'. Two other collections of his poems are: *En la calle de en medio* and *Poemas para el año del elefante*. After the Revolution he became Sandinista ambassador to Maputo. His poem 'When it Rains' is published in *Poesía Libre* 19.

Carlos Martínez Rivas   Pages: 210-3

Born 1924, poet, art critic and diplomat, he was a member of the '1940 Generation' of poets, together with Ernesto Cardenal. His poetry collection *La Insurrecíon solitaria* first published in 1953 was re-issued by ENN in 1982. Much of his post-Revolution poetry attacks right wing catholicism and the hierarchy.

Welcome, Monseñor   Pages: 210-3

Pope John Paul II visited Managua in March 1983. At a large public meeting mothers begged the Pope to bless their sons who had just been killed by the Contras. When the Pope ignored the women, the crowd echoed their request until, apparently irate, he shouted, 'Silence! Silence!'. The Pope also admonished Ernesto Cardenal, Minister of Culture, for disobeying papal orders to resign his post in the Sandinista government. In 1985 the Pope appointed the conservative archbishop of Managua, Monseñor Obando y Bravo, the only cardinal in Central America. The poem refers to the reception for this occasion.

Luis Alfonso Velásquez: a child who helped the Sandinista guerrillas. A park is called after him in Managua.

Luis Enrique Mejía Godoy   Pages: 88-9

Luis Enrique and Carlos Mejía Godoy are the two brother singer-songwriters who composed the *Canto Epico to the FSLN* – a song cycle telling the whole story of the revolution beginning in 1927 with Sandino's 'crazy little army' and ending with the triumph on July 19th 1979 (translated in *The Nicaraguan Epic*, Katabasis, London 1989). Luis Enrique began writing songs attacking the dictatorship in the sixties. Among his best known songs about Sandino are 'Si Adelita se fuera con otro', 'Allá va el General', 'Compañero Cesar'. His song 'Venancia' composed in 1974 is dedicated to all the children who were couriers and guides for the FSLN. With his brother Carlos he composed *Guitarra Armada*, one of whose songs '¿Qué es el FAL?' gives instructions on how to use this gun. Their songs acted as an inspiration during the revolutionary struggle and were broadcast on the clandestine Radio Sandino. After the triumph Luis Enrique with his band Mancotal made frequent tours abroad to tell people about the Revolution and raise money for Nicaragua.

Revenge   Pages: 88-9

This song is based on words by Tomás Borge to his torturers. The chorus of the song is:

And it was the people that hated you most
when songs were of violence and dread
but the people under their skin
have hearts beating black and red.

When Tomás became Sandinista Minister of the Interior he met his torturers again and revenged himself by forgiving them. In view of his position as Minister, he also asked for the rape and murder of his first wife Yelba not to be taken into account in the trial of the National Guardsmen responsible.

José Mendoza   Pages: 168-9

FSLN combatant, who became a soldier in the EPS (Sandinista People's Army), and fell in combat defending the country against the Contras in 1988.

Vidaluz Meneses   Pages: 226-231

Born in Matagalpa in 1944, convent-educated, her father was a member of Somoza's National Guard. After the Revolution she worked with Ernesto Cardenal and others to set up the new Ministry of Culture. She also worked in the Sandinista Association of Cultural Workers (ASTC). At present she is head of the Department of Arts and Letters in Faculty of Humanities of the Central American University (UCA) in Managua. She has published: *Llama Guardada* (Managua 1975); *El aire que me llama* (Imelsa, Managua 1982); *Llama en el aire* (ENN, Managua 1991: from which the two poems translated here are taken). A selection of her poems appears in the anthology *La mujer nicaragüense en la poesía* (ENN, Managua 1992). Some of her poems are translated in *Lovers and Comrades* (London 1989), including her best known poem, 'Last Postcard to my Father, General Meneses'.

Ricardo Morales Avilés   Pages: 62-71

Born 1939, he was a university teacher and Sandinista militant. From 1966 he was engaged in 'semi-legal' and clandestine activities under the command of Julio Buitrago, chief of the FSLN urban guerrillas in Managua. Captured on 12th September 1968, for three years Ricardo made his cell in La Aviación prison a 'revolution workshop', writing countless articles, engaging in debates. Most of his prose is polemical or political analysis, most of his poems are love poems to Doris Tijerino. Released on 4th October 1971, he became a member of the

FSLN leadership during the period of 'silent accumulation of forces'. On 17th September 1973 he was captured by the National Guard in Nandaime, together with Oscar Turcios. Next day their severely tortured dead bodies were found. A verse of Carlos Mejía's song 'No se me raje mi compa' recalls how the Guard who tortured Ricardo was frightened by the sparks in his big shining eyes and the only words they could get out of him were: 'Soy y seré militante de la causa sandinista': 'I am and I will be a militant for the Sandinista cause.' The two poems translated here are both in Ricardo Morales Avilés, *Obras: No pararemos de andar jamás* (ENN, Managua 1983). The poems are addressed to his *compañera*, Doris Tijerino, also a Sandinista militant from the early sixties. She was captured in the siege of the safe house near the Delicias del Volga in Managua on July 15th 1969. Julio Buitrago was killed, Doris was caught when she managed to get a child out of the house. Doris was tortured, released, captured again in April 1978, released on 22nd August 1978 as a result of the Assault on the Palace. After the Revolution she became head of the Sandinista police. In the 1990 elections she was returned as FSLN deputy for Matagalpa. (See also Doris Tijerino, *Inside the Nicaraguan Revolution* (New Star Books, Vancouver 1978).

Rosario Murillo   Pages: 290-3

Born in Managua in 1951, she was assistant to Pedro Joaquín Chamorro on the newspaper *La Prensa* and worked closely with its literary editor, Pablo Antonio Cuadra. In 1974 she founded the *Gradas* group, which worked through popular culture to oppose the dictator. After the Revolution she became Secretary General of the Sandinista Association of Cultural Workers (ASTC) and co-ordinator of *Ventana*, the cultural supplement to the newspaper *Barricada*, which initiated a critical debate on the value of the workshop poetry in March 1981. In the 1984 elections she was elected as an FSLN member of the National Assembly. Her publications include *Un Deber de Cantar* (Ministry of Culture, Managua 1982), *En las espléndidas ciudades* (ENN, Managua 1985), from which the poem translated here is taken, and *Las esperanzas misteriosas* (Vanguardia, Managua 1990). She appears in the anthology of six Nicaraguan women poets *A puro Golpe de Amor* (Casa de las Imagenes, Mexico City 1989) and the anthology *La Mujer Nicaragüense en la Poesía* (Managua 1992).

Some of her work is translated in *Lovers and Comrades* (London 1989). She is married to Daniel Ortega.

Michèle Najlis   Pages: 38-9

Born 1946, she studied at the National University. Her political activities drove her into exile for 7 years. She returned with the triumph of the revolution, worked for the Ministry of the Interior as Head of Media. She also wrote journalism and made cultural programmes for television. From 1985 she worked for the Ministry of Education and wrote some text books. Her published works include *El viento armado* (1969), *Ars combinatoria* (1987), *Cantos de Ifigenia* (1991). Her poems appear in *La mujer nicaragüense en la Poesía* (Managua 1992) and in translation in *Lovers and Comrades* (London 1989). The poem translated here is published in PPN.

Daniel Ortega   Pages: 44-9

Born in 1945, Daniel Ortega joined the student protest group JPN (Patriotic Nicaraguan Youth) in 1960 at the age of 14 and the FSLN in 1963. He was arrested and tortured in 1964 and again in 1967, when he was sentenced to 20 years imprisonment. He was released with other political prisoners following the successful action led by Eduardo Contreras on December 27th 1974. Ortega was one of the leaders of the *Tercerista* (Third) or Insurrectionary tendency of the FSLN, whose strategy prevailed when the the three tendencies finally united in March 1979 in a common effort to overthrow the dictator Somoza. With the triumph of the Revolution, Ortega became co-ordinator of the new 5-person Government Junta of National Reconstruction. In the 1984 elections the FSLN gained 67% of the vote and Ortega was elected President of Nicaragua. In February 1990 the FSLN was defeated by the US-backed coalition UNO, led by Violeta Chamorro, and Ortega handed over the presidency to her. Daniel Ortega is married to Rosario Murillo.

In Prison Pages: 44-9

The poem was written in prison between 1967 and 1974 (the time when miniskirts were in fashion). It is published in PPN.

Cony Pacheco Pages: 186-7

Born León 1957, she is a nurse. She helped set up the poetry workshops and led the workshop in Subtiava, the Indian *barrio* of León. She was on the editorial board of *Poesía Libre* and some of her poems appeared in it. She also has poems in the anthologies *Talleres de Poesía* (Ministry of Culture, Managua 1983: from which the poem translated here is taken); *La mujer nicaragüense en la poesía* (Managua 1992) and translated in *Lovers and Comrades* (London 1989).

Felipe Peña Pages: 94-101

It is thought he was born in 1954. He was a peasant member of Ernesto Cardenal's community in the Solentiname islands on Lake Nicaragua, where he belonged to the poetry workshop. On 13th October 1977, after taking part in the attack on the San Carlos National Guard barracks, he was captured and imprisoned, released with fifty-eight others through the FSLN Assault on the National Palace on August 22nd 1978. Thereafter he rejoined the FSLN guerrillas in Nueva Guinea, in the south east of Nicaragua, and was killed in May 1979. Some of his poems are published in *Poesía campesina de Solentiname* (Ministry of Culture, Managua 1980) and in bi-lingual text in *The Peasant Poets of Solentiname* (London 1991).

Liberation Day Pages: 94-5

When the political prisoners were released as a result of the Assault on the Palace, huge crowds lined the route to the Managua airport, whence they flew to Panama.

A Good Leader   Pages: 98-101

Gaspar García Laviana born in 1941, son of a miner in Asturias, Spain, spent many years as a worker priest in Madrid. He spent four years doing building work and trying to minister to the poor in Nicaragua but came to feel he was 'more a servant of the Somoza tyranny and a lackey of that corrupt regime', so he joined the FSLN as a combatant and was killed in action on December 11th 1978. His poems *Cantos de Amor y guerra* were published by the Ministry of Culture in 1979. There is a song about him on the cassette *Guitarra Armada*.

El Danto: ('The Tapir') was the nickname of Germán Pomares Ordoñez, veteran FSLN militant. He was killed on May 24th 1979, leading the attack on Jinotega.

Sergio Ramírez   Pages: 40-3, 242-3

Born 1942, he studied law at León University, where he took part in the student demonstration on 23rd July 1959, during which the Guard open-fired and killed four students. In 1960, together with Fernando Gordillo, he founded the *Frente Ventana*, with a literary magazine that was committed to opposing the dictator. In 1977 he co-ordinated *Los Doce*, the 'Group of Twelve' prominent persons, including priests and businessmen who openly supported the FSLN in a statement issued from San José Costa Rica and published in in *La Prensa* in November 1977. With the triumph of the Revolution Sergio Ramírez represented *Los Doce* on the 5-person Government Junta of National Reconstruction. After the FSLN election victory in 1984, he became Vice President of Nicaragua. He is known primarily as a novelist and short story writer. His novel *To Bury Our Fathers* and his *Stories* (trans. Nick Caistor, Readers International, London 198)6 are among his works published in English. His *Confesión de Amor* (Nicarao, Managua 1991) is an autobiographical account written after the 1990 election defeat. The Postscript to this anthology is an extract from it. The poem 'After you Fled' is published in PPN.

Confession of Love, extract   Pages: 242-3

Eduardo Contreras ('Comandante Marcos') led the Juan José Quezada commando raid on Chema Castillo's house on 27th December 1974. He died in action on the Managua-León road on 7th November 1976.

Camilo Ortega, brother of Daniel and Humberto, was sent by the FSLN to support the insurrection in Monimbó in February 1978. He was killed on 26th February 1978 in Las Sabogales, Masaya.

Israel Lewites, FSLN militant who was killed in the October Offensive of 1977 in Masaya.

Luis Rocha   Pages: 132-3

Born 1945, a poet and journalist, he is the co-ordinator of *Nuevo Amanecer Cultural*, the weekly cultural supplement of the newspaper *El Nuevo Diario*. He is a member of the National Assembly. He has published 3 collections: *Domus aurea*; *Ejercicios de composición*; and *Phocas* (ENN, Managua 1983), from which the poem 'Against the Light' is taken.

Lesbia Rodríguez   Pages: 164-7

During the 1980 Literacy Campaign she taught in San Isidro de Bolas. Her 'Poem to a Civil Defence Member' appears in the collection of poems by literacy teachers *Fogata en la oscurana* (Ministry of Culture, Managua 1985). She belonged to the Bello Horizonte poetry workshop in Managua and her 'Reflection upon Reading a Poem' appears in *Poesía Libre* 17 (August 1986).

Poem to a Civil Defence Member   Pages: 164-5

The word 'Cedecista' in the Spanish title means member of the CDS, Sandinista Defence Committee, local organisations that co-ordinated civil defence, food distribution and other community tasks.

Reflection upon Reading a Poem   Pages: 166-7

The poet Edwin Castro, imprisoned for complicity in the killing of the
dictator Somoza by Rigoberto López Pérez, was murdered in prison
by the National Guard on May 18th 1960.

Luis Alfonso Velásquez was a Sandinista child hero, who had this
park in Managua named after him.

ANS: Association of Sandinista Children.
'Los Carlitos': a children's group named after Carlos Fonseca.

Leonel Rugama   Pages: 52-61

Born March 21st 1949 near Estelí, he left the seminary where he was
studying to be a priest to join the FSLN urban guerrillas in Managua.
On January 15th 1970 the National Guard surrounded the safe house
where he was staying in the Cementerio Oriental District of Managua
with troops, tanks and helicopters. When called upon by the Guard to
surrender, Leonel replied with the defiant insult: '¡Que se rinda tu
madre!': ('Let your mother surrender!') and fought on till he was
killed. The battle is described graphically in Ernesto Cardenal's poem
'Oracle over Managua' translated by Donald D. Walsh in Ernesto
Cardenal, *Zero Hour and other Documentary Poems* (New Directions,
New York, 1980). Teófilo Cabastrero has published a biography
Leonel Rugama: El Delito de Tomar la Vida en Serio (Editorial Nueva
Nicaragua, Managua 1989). In Carlos Mejía Godoy's *Canto Epico to
the FSLN* and his song 'No se me Raje, mi compa' ('Comrade, don't
let me down'), Leonel Rugama 'committed the enormous crime of
taking life seriously'.

The Earth is a Satellite of the Moon   Pages: 52-5

The US astronauts Armstrong and Aldrin trod on the moon on June
21st 1969, leaving their footprints in its thick dust. They broadcast to
earth.

Acahualinca: A very poor *barrio* of Managua, where the capital's
sewage went into the lake. In this *barrio* are to be found the *Huellas de
Acahualinca*: Indian footprints preserved in volcanic rock. In another

satirical poem Leonel speaks of all the seminarians going for a walk to the *Huellas de Acahualinca.*

The Houses Remained Full of Smoke   Pages: 56-9

Julio Buitrago, the leader of the FSLN in Managua, was killed on July 15th 1969 in the safe house near the Delicias del Volga in Managua. The other three comrades the poem is dedicated to were killed on the same day in a house in the Santo Domingo district.

Epitafio   Pages: 60-1

The line 'with no alternative but the struggle' expresses the position reached by many Nicaraguans in the 70s, including christians, who had been reluctant to resort to arms to overthrow the dictator.

Fernando Silva   Pages: 34-5

Born 1927, poet and story writer, he describes himself as 'the most Nicaraguan man on earth'. Among his published works are 2 books of stories, *Cuentos* and *Puertos y Cuentos* (both ENN, Managua 1986). He is a doctor specialising in pediatrics and director of the Managua Children's Hospital. In 1986 the Ministry of Culture published his book of information, poems and cartoons about child health: *La Salud del Niño*, helping to popularise Sandinista public health measures. His poem 'Epigram' is published in PPN.

Epigram   Pages: 34-5

La Prensa was the pre-Revolution bourgeois opposition newspaper owned and edited by Pedro Joaquín Chamorro. After the Revolution it became violently anti-Sandinista.

Dora María Téllez   Pages: 90-3

Born 1955, she became a Sandinista *guerrillera* with rank of *comandante*. She was 'Comandante Dos' [2: i.e. third in command after 0 and 1] in the Assault on the Palace on August 22nd 1978. After the Revolution she became Minister of Health in the Sandinista government and a member of the National Assembly. In the 1990 elections she was re-elected as an FSLN deputy to the National Assembly. See also Daisy Zamora's poem about her on pages 124-5.

Isidro Tercero   Pages: 188-9

FSLN combatant. Isidro Tercero is a pseudonym because he was a member of the Sandinista state security (intelligence) service and belonged to its poetry workshop. His poems appear in the anthologies *Talleres de Poesía* (1983: from which the poem translated here is taken) and *Poesía de las Fuerzas Armadas* (1985) (both Ministry of Culture, Managua).

José Coronel Urtecho   Pages: 134-43

Born in Granada in 1906, he is a very influential poet in Nicaragua, also essayist and translator of US poetry (with Ernesto Cardenal, his nephew). He founded the Vanguard literary movement in 1927, which explored new poetic forms and Nicaraguan folklore but was politically uncommitted. Urtecho later described the movement as 'a sort of literary playboyism'. He created the term 'exteriorism' for the kind of poetry particularly favoured by himself and Ernesto Cardenal. For more than 30 years he has lived in the rural Río San Juan region. His collected prose was published as *Prosa reunida* (ENN, Managua 1985). His collected poems were published as *Pol-la d'ananta katanta paranta* (UNAN, Nicaragua 1987). His three long revolutionary poems are: *Conversación con Carlos* (Vanguardia, Managua 1986); Paneles de Infierno (translated by John Lyons: *Panels of Hell* (Arts for Nicaragua, London 1989); and *No volverá el pasado*, translated here.

The Past Will Not Return   Pages: 134-43

Bitterly for the Sandinistas, the title of this poem was used for a song in their 1990 election campaign.

Julio Valle-Castillo   Pages: 215-225

Born in Masaya in 1952, he studied in Mexico, where he published his two first collections of poetry, *Las armas iniciales* (1977) and *Formas migratorias* (1979), and engaged in solidarity work for Nicaragua. He returned to Nicaragua after the Revolution and worked in the Ministry of Culture. He was the editor of its poetry magazine *Poesía Libre*. He is on the editorial board of *Nuevo Amanecer Cultural*. His collection *Materia jubilosa* was published by ENN in 1986 and 21 of these poems are available in a bi-lingual text collected as 'Nicaraguan Vision and other Poems' in *The Nicaraguan Epic* (Katabasis, London 1989). This publication coincided with a reading by the poet in the Purcell Room in London.

The Passion according to the Neighbours   Pages: 214-9

For José Mendoza, see above and his poem on pages 168-9.

Ballad of the Deserter   Pages: 220-3

Military Service: Conscription was introduced in August 1983 to defend the country from Contra attacks and against a possible US invasion.

Postcard to Captain Bosco Centeno   Pages: 224-5

For Bosco Centeno, see above and his poem 'To Chicha (Tony) who Fell in Nueva Guinea' on pages 158-9.

Arlen Siu was an FSLN militant of Chinese descent, who was killed in action at El Sauce in 1975, covering her comrades' retreat. She was a poet and singer – her most famous song was 'Maria Rural' about the hardship suffered by Nicaragua's peasant women. Carlos Mejía Godoy's song about her is on the cassette *Guitarra Armada* and Julio Valle-Castillo has a poem about her translated in *The Nicaraguan Epic*.

Miklós Radnóti wrote some Postcard poems. A selection of Radnóti's poetry is published in *Against Forgetting: Twentieth Century Poetry of Witness*, ed. Carolyn Forché (W.W. Norton, USA 1993).

Daisy Zamora   Pages: 124-131

Born in Managua in 1950, Daisy Zamora was educated in convents, became actively involved with the FSLN in the seventies. She was part of the support network for the Assault on the Palace in August 1978 and hid half the FSLN squad in her house. She worked with the clandestine Radio Sandino. After the Revolution she became Vice Minister of Culture and head of the North American Desk at the Sandinista Department of International Relations. At present she is the Sor Juana de la Cruz professor of literature at the Central American University (UCA) in Managua. She has published two collections of poetry *La violenta espuma* (Ministry of Culture, Managua, 1982) and En limpio se escribe la vida (ENN, Managua 1988) and edited an anthology of Nicaraguan women poets, *La mujer nicaragüense en la poesía* (ENN, Managua 1992). Some of her poems are translated in *Lovers and Comrades* (London 1989). A collection of her poems in bilingual text is forthcoming from Katabasis.

Comandante Dos   Pages: 124-5

is published in *La violenta espuma*.

For Dora María Téllez see above and her poem on page 90. Dora María was 'Comandante Dos' in the Assault on the Palace. The FSLN squad wore 'borrowed' uniforms of the EEBI (Basic Infantry Training School), the elite counter-insurgency National Guard troops commanded by the dictator's son 'Tacho' Somoza.

50 Lines of Love and an Unmet Confession...   Pages: 126-31

is published in *En limpio se escribe la vida*.

Ernesto: For Ernesto Cardenal and his part in the April Conspiracy of 1954, see above.
Julio: Julio Valle-Castillo (see above).